ARABIC
FOLKTALES
FOR LANGUAGE LEARNERS

Traditional Stories in Arabic and English

ARABIC FOLKTALES

FOR LANGUAGE LEARNERS

حكايات شعبية عربية لمتعلمي اللغة

Sarah Risha

TUTTLE Publishing

Tokyo | Rutland, Vermont | Singapore

Contents

Introduction

One of the best ways to learn about a culture is through its folktales. This book includes a collection of well-known folktales from the Arab world that are much loved by the young and old generations. These stories are selected from a variety of resources. They reflect cultural, social, and religious aspects of Arabic culture and provide practical lessons of life. As in all folktales, they offer advice to overcome difficulties and share valid lessons from the experiences of others. The stories are simplified and edited for teaching purposes. Each story has a simple plot with few characters.

Some of the stories reflect the origins of popular proverbs, others use familiar characters and powerful leaders who serve as a judges or wise men to provide keen solutions for problems while others are rooted firmly in the imagination. Also, because the Arab world is so vast, they may vary from one country to another depending on the traditions and culture of its people. Every story in this book has its own value and unique lesson. In ancient times, these stories were told from one generation to the next orally. I have wonderful memories of my grandma telling me bedtime stories. She did not use a book; the stories she recited from memory were handed down to her from her own grandparents. The stories in this book reflect the rich tradition of Arab storytelling.

Folktales are a powerful tool for teaching and promoting critical thinking. Also, reading interesting stories can be a very effective way of learning a language as they are effective at attractively conveying values and morals. Even religious texts use storytelling to teach their followers the lessons they need to learn and apply. Many parents might lose their voices screaming at their children to teach them values and make them respect their rules. However, using storytelling may make this process much easier and at the same time engaging for both parents and children.

In general, culture may be defined as the inherited traditions, values, customs, etiquette, and practices of a society. It encompasses a wide range of aspects including stories, proverbs, poems, holidays, celebrations, and even dances. Arab countries share many cultural aspects, but at the same time, each country has its own unique folktales, culture, and traditions that are passed down from generation to generation.

As with most folktales, each story is designed to introduce the reader to Arab culture while at the same time, helping reinforce language skills in an entertaining way for beginning and intermediate learners.

كان يا مكان means "once upon a time" and في قديم الزمان means "in the old days." Most Arabic stories use both or one of these expressions when start telling a story.

About This Book

Stories

The book contains 28 stories with different lengths. At the beginning of this book, the reader is presented with simple, one-paragraph stories followed by slightly longer stories of two to three paragraphs. They become increasingly longer and more detailed with more complex sentences and vocabulary as the book progresses. Each story is presented in Arabic and English on facing pages. Vocabulary lists will be provided at the end of each story.

Arabic Text

The Arabic language has diverse dialects that vary from one country (or region) to another. However, Modern Standard Arabic, which is used in this book, plays an important role in connecting people throughout the Arab world. Modern Standard Arabic is taught in all schools in all Arab countries. It is the language of print media and TV. The stories introduced in this book are simplified and some are shortened to make them more suitable for beginner and intermediate levels.

English Text

English text is provided under each story, or paragraph for longer ones. This is to reinforce an understanding of the Arabic text.

Glossary

An English-Arabic glossary is provided at the end of the book.

For Each Story

New vocabulary is introduced in Arabic and English at the end of each story. Stories are introduced followed by translation. After each story, discussion questions will help reinforce the reader's understanding of the content and vocabulary.

Grammar

Simple grammar that can be learned is discussed and presented in the Introduction so the reader may refer to it whenever needed. For example, sentences in Arabic might be verbal, starting with a verb, or nominal starting with a noun or a pronoun. In Arabic, as in other languages, verbs are conjugated according to the subject, that is, verbs might be singular, dual, or plural depending on the subject. Additionally, verbs may be present, past, or future tense.

Vocabulary and Expressions

To make things easier, new vocabulary and expressions are introduced before the Arabic texts.

Cultural Notes

This section introduces the message of each story and its relation to Arab culture.

For example, Arabs commonly shake hands when they meet each other. Also, male friends kiss their male friends and female friends kiss their female friends on the cheeks. Young people kiss their elder relatives, fathers, mothers, grandmothers, grandfathers, uncles, and aunts on their hands or on their heads. Hugs are also very common. Therefore, when a story describes a son kissing his father's head, this tradition will be explained before the story.

Comprehension and Language

The book starts with short simple stories to longer and more complicated ones. Vocabulary forms are presented and explained. Additionally, common expressions are noted. The goal is to develop reading and comprehension skills

Discussion Points

Usually, questions and discussion points help the reader learn more, therefore there will be a few comprehension questions after each story, depending on the length, to reinforce language usage and interpretation. These questions will help develop an appreciation for each story, explore its hidden message, and relate them to the reader's own life. The last question in most stories is often designed to elicit your opinion or what you have learned from the story. This encourages critical thinking and helps you practice expressing your ideas and opinions in the Arabic language.

Online Audio Files

The stories are available as free downloadable online audio recorded by native Arabic and English speakers.

Illustrations

Each story will be accompanied by illustrations that picture scenes from the stories. Visual learners will especially appreciate the illustrations as learning aids.

How to Use This Book

Before you start reading the story, it is a good idea to read and learn the new vocabulary of each story. Do some practice by using the words, especially new vocabulary, in a sentence of your own. Then read the story and check your understanding by reading the translation. Lastly, read the discussion questions and use your own words and some of the new words you learned to answer the questions.

The Arabic Language

Grammar

Learning grammar is crucial in understanding any language. The Arabic Language is considered to be one of the oldest languages and is spoken by over 400 million people, making it the fifth most widely spoken language in the world. Arabic is also of significant value to Muslims as it is the language of the Qur'an, the holy book of Islam. Therefore, many non-Arabs are learning the language to understand the Qur'an. It is recommended to spend time studying the grammar, practice using your own examples, and apply what you have learned to enhance your understanding of the language.

Here are some important rules you may notice through reading.

Sentences

There are two kinds of sentences in Arabic:

- Nominal sentences: sentences starting with a noun or a pronoun.
- Verbal sentences: ones starting with a verb.

Negating Sentences

The following four particles are used to negate sentences and each of them has its own use:

- لَم is used to negate verbal sentences when the verb is in present tense as in: لم يدرس التلميذ = the student did not study. Note the verb is in present tense but the meaning is in the past tense.
- لَن is used to negate verbal sentences when you are talking about the future as in: لن يدرس التلميذ = the student will not study. Note the verb is in the present tense but the meaning is in the future tense.

- مَا is used to negate verbal sentences when the verb is in past tense as in: مَا درس التلميذ = the student did not study. The verb here is in the past tense
- ليس is used to negate nominal sentences as in: ليس عندي كتاب

Gender in Arabic

All words in the Arabic language are either feminine or masculine including words referring to things. To recognize the gender of the words, there are some very simple and general rules regarding feminine words:

1. Words refer to feminine people as mother, sister, girl ...etc.
2. All words ending in **ta marbuta** are considered feminine words, even the ones referring to things as in: مكتبة- طاوله – سيارة.
3. Names of almost all countries, villages, and cities are considered feminine.
4. Some words ending in ـاء as in سماء (sky) and صحراء (desert) are considered feminine. However please pay attention that some plural words end with ـاء as in علماء the plural of masculine word عالم scholar and فقراء the plural of فقير poor and they are not feminine words. This rule applies to words referring to singular only.
5. Words ending in **alif maqsoora** ى are considered feminine as in: صغرى (small) and عطشى(thirsty).

However, some feminine words do not follow these rules. For example:

شمس sun
ريح wind
يد hand
عين eye

Numbers

The Arabic language has masculine and feminine forms of numbers. The numbers 1 and 2 should match what we are talking about while the numbers 3–10 should be the opposite. For example:

سيارة واحدة

كتاب واحد

خمس سيارات

ثلاثة كتب

Here are the numbers from 1–10:

English #	Arabic #	Number (F)	Number (M)
1	١	واحدة	واحد
2	٢	اثنتان	اثنان
3	٣	ثلاثة	ثلاث
4	٤	أربعة	أربع
5	٥	خمسة	خمس
6	٦	ستة	ست
7	٧	سبعة	سبع
8	٨	ثمانية	ثمان
9	٩	تسعة	تسع
10	١٠	عشرة	عشر
0	٠		صفر

On a side note, it is well known that the numerals used in English numbers are Arabic numbers. They were developed by the Arabs during the tenth century and spread into Europe. However, the numbers that are used in the Arab world are originally Indian numbers.

Colors

In the Arabic language, we have masculine and feminine forms of colors, and they should match what we are describing. If we are describing a masculine noun, then the color should be masculine and when we are describing a feminine noun then the color should be feminine.

In the table below M refers to the masculine form and F refers to the feminine form.

Meaning	Color (F)	Color (M)
White	بيضاء	أبيض
Black	سوداء	أسود
Red	حمراء	أحمر
Blue	زرقاء	أزرق
Green	خضراء	أخضر
Yellow	صفراء	أصفر
Brown	بنّيه	بني
Orange	برتقالية	برتقالي
Purple	بنفسجية	بنفسجي
Grey	رمادية	رمادي
Pink	وردية	وردي
Silver	فضية	فضي
Gold	ذهبية	ذهبي

Did you notice that feminine forms end in either **ta marbuta** or **alif** and **hamza**?

The Definite Article

In Arabic to define a noun we add **al** ال at the beginning of the word. It is the same as writing "a" or "the" before a noun. For example: كتاب means "book" but if I write: الكتاب then it means "the book."

As in English, we cannot add **al** to proper nouns or names of people. Some Arab countries have **al** as part of their names as in: الكويت — الجزائر — السعودية & البحرين. Some countries do not have **al** as in: قطر — دبي — and مصر. ليبيا

Prepositions

It is good to know that all nouns that come after a preposition should have **kasra**. Here is a list of the prepositions:

Meaning	Preposition
At / in	فـي
To	إلى
Belongs to	لِ
From	مـن

Meaning	Preposition
On	عـلـى
With, by	بـ
With	مع
About	عن

Question Words

Here is the list of question words:

Meaning	Question word
Where	أين
When	متى
Is, are, was/were Do, does, did	هل
What (followed by nouns)	ما
What (followed by verbs)	ماذا
Who	مَن
How	كيف
How many/ much	كم
Which	أي

Adjectives

There is only one important rule for all adjectives which is: they should follow the noun we are describing.

- Adjectives should follow the gender of the noun we are describing. When describing masculine nouns then the adjective should be masculine and when describing feminine nouns then the adjective should be feminine as in: سيارة كبيرة – شارع واسع
- In dual nouns, adjectives should be dual as in: بيتان صغيران – أختان طويلتان
- For plurals, when we are describing human plurals then the adjective should be plural and match in gender as in: رجال محترمين – بنات صغيرات
- However, when describing non-human plural then the adjective should be in singular feminine form as in: شوارع واسعة – جامعات كبيرة

Weekdays

The words "أسبوع" and "يوم" are used as masculine words when used as singular or dual. So, I would say: هذا يوم – هذا أسبوع – هذان يومان – هذان اسبوعان

However, when "أسبوع" and "يوم" are used in the plural they are considered feminine nouns. It should be: هذه أسابيع and هذه أيام

The names of the days of the week are masculine all the time.

Here are the weekdays:

Meaning	Plural	Weekday
Week	أسابيع	أسبوع
Day	أيام	يوم
Saturday		السبت
Sunday		الأحد
Monday		الاثنين

Meaning	Plural	Weekday
Tuesday		الثلاثاء
Wednesday		الأربعاء
Thursday		الخميس
Friday		الجمعة

Seasons

The names of the seasons are considered masculine nouns. The word "season" فصل is masculine in singular and dual forms but considered feminine in plural.

The four seasons are:

Meaning	Word
Season	فصل فصول (plural)
Summer	الصيف
Spring	الربيع
Winter	الشتاء
Autumn	الخريف

Verb Forms

Verbs are conjugated according to the person or pronoun we are talking about. Here is a list of conjugated verbs and these conjugations apply to all verbs.

Verb in past tense	ذهب went	لاحظ noticed	عمل did	مسك held	كشف uncover
أنا أ	أذهب	ألاحظ	أعمل	أمسك	نكشف
نحن ن	نذهب	نلاحظ	نعمل	نمسك	أكشف
أنتَ ت	تذهب	تلاحظ	تعمل	تمسك	تكشف
أنت ت ..... ين	تذهبين	تلاحظين	تعملين	تمسكين	تكشفين

Verb in past tense	ذهب went	لاحظ noticed	عمل did	مسك held	كشف uncover
أنتم ت.......ون	تذهبون	تلاحظون	تعملون	تمسكون	تكشفون
هو ي.......	يذهب	يلاحظ	يعمل	يمسك	يكشف
هي ت......	تذهب	تلاحظ	تعمل	تمسك	تكشف
هم ي.....ون	يذهبون	يلاحظون	يعملون	يمسكون	يكشفون

Future Tense Verbs

It is very easy to conjugate the verb into future tense. All you need to do is add **a** ‑س at the beginning of the present tense verb. For example:

سيلاحظ Would be يلاحظ
سأكتب Would be أكتب
سيمسك Would be يمسك
سيعرفون Would be يعرفون
ستذهبين Would be تذهبين
ستحضر Would be تحضر

Another option is to use the word سوف (will/ shall) before the verb. For example:

سوف يدرس – سوف تذهبين & سوف يحضرون

The Dual Form in Arabic

As you know, plural refers to three or more people or things. The Arabic language uses the dual form referring to two nouns, verbs, adjectives or things. It is called "**mothanna**" in Arabic.

We have two pronouns for the dual form: أنتما and هما. They are used for both masculine and feminine.

For verbs in the present tense, just add "**an**" at the end of the verb as in:

يكتبان would be يكتب
يذهبان would be يذهب

For the past tense, add just an "**aa**" at the end of the verb·

فتحا would be فتح
درسا would be درس

To change a singular noun or adjective into the dual form, you just add the suffix "**an**" or "**en**" to the end of the word. Some examples are:

كتابين - كتابان would be كتاب
بيتان - بيتين would be بيت
استاذين استاذان would be أستاذ

If the word ends in **ta marbuta** then change it into regular **ta** and do the same, that is add "**an**" or "**en**"

Here are some examples:

حديقتان حديقتين would be حديقة
معلمتين معلمتان would be معلمة
كبيرتين كبيرتان would be كبيرة

The good news is that there is no broken dual, so all words can be changed into dual using the description above.

Noun Conjugation According to the subject

Nouns are conjugated according to what you are talking about or the subject of the sentences. For example, in English, we use different pronouns for the people we are talking about as I, you, …etc. In Arabic, we conjugate the noun according to the person or thing I am talking about. In the following table, you will find the conjugation of two words, the first is a masculine word (book) and the second is a feminine word (room) ending in **ta marbuta**. Notice how we changed the **ta marbuta** into regular **ta** and added whatever we needed after it. This applies to all nouns.

Example	Changes	Meaning	Pronoun
كتابي – غرفتي	ي.....	I	أنا
كتابنا – غرفتنا	نا.....	We	نحن
كتابكَ – غرفتكَ	كَ.....	You (M)	أنتَ
كتابك – غرفتك	ك.....	You (F)	أنت
كتابكم – غرفتكم	كم.....	You (Plural)	أنتم
كتابه – غرفته	ـه / ه.....	He	هو
كتابها – غرفتها	ها/ ـها.....	She	هي
كتابهما	هما.....	They (Dual)	هما
كتابهم	هم.....	They (Plural)	هم

The Stories

جحا و العالم
Joha and the Scholar

Cultural Note

Joha is a well-known figure in Arab folktales. He is famous for his wit, intelligence, tricks, and foolishness. Despite being poor, he gave the impression of being superior to others and used his unique lifestyle to solve problems creatively and distinctively. Joha's stories have been passed down from generation to generation and are widely told throughout the Arab world. Not only are they entertaining, but they also serve as a means of teaching values and promoting critical thinking. Children and adults alike enjoy listening to Joha's tales, and his stories are often used to bring a smile to people's faces. The character of Joha is a cherished part of Arab culture and continues to be an important part of the region's literary heritage.

Translation

Once a scholar went to the area where Joha lived. He heard about Joha and his intuitiveness, so he felt jealous and wanted to challenge him in front of his people. So, he called Joha to a contest, and Joha agreed. The scholar's intention was to embarrass Joha and to prove that he is the intelligent one and that people should seek his advice when they need any.

On the appointed day, the scholar called everyone in the area and told Joha, "I will ask you forty questions. You must give the same answer to all questions."

Joha considered this an easy contest and said, "Ask whatever you want!"

The scholar was surprised and started his questions. When he was done, Joha smiled and said, "I have one answer for all forty questions."

The scholar was very shocked and asked, "What is your answer?"

Joha said, "I don't know."

في يوم من الأيام جاء عالِم مشهور إلى المنطقة التي يعيش فيها جحا. سمع العالم عن جحا وسرعة بديهته فشعر بالغيرة منه و أراد أن يتحداه أمام قومه ليثبت لهم أنه أذكى من جحا. أعلن العالِم عن تحديه و دعا كل من في المنطقة أن يحضر ليثبت لهم أنه هو العالِم و يجب أن يسألوه هو ما يحتاجون و ليس جحا.

و في اليوم المحدد قال العالِم لجحا أمام جميع أهل القرية : أريد أن أسألك أربعين سؤالا و يجب أن تجيب عليها كلها.

وافق جحا و قال له اسأل ما تريد.

تفاجأ العالِم بجواب جحا و بدأ يسأل أسئلته .و بعد أن انتهى من الأربعين سؤالا. قال له جحا: عندي جواب واحد لكل أسئلتك .

قال العالم مستغربا: ما هو ؟ قال جحا: لا أعرف !

Vocabulary

Meaning	Plural	Word
Scholar	علماء	عالِم
Famous	مشهورين	مشهور
The area	مناطق	منطقة
Intuitiveness		بديهه
Challenge		يتحدى
Jealousy		غيرة
Prove		يثبت

Meaning	Plural	Word
I know		أعرف
Question	أسئلة	سؤال
The same		نفس
Shocked		تفاجأ
Response		اجابة
Surprised		مستغربا

المناقشة:

1. لماذا أراد العالِم أن يتحدى جحا؟

2. كم سؤالا سأل العالِم جحا؟

3. ما رأيك في جواب جحا؟

جحا و الشكوى
Joha and Complaining

Cultural Note

People from all cultures, not only Arabs, work hard to achieve their goals and make a good impression on others. In Arab culture, people avoid complaining publicly and instead only confide in close friends, because they do not want to give the wrong impression about themselves or their difficulties. The story of Joha teaches an important lesson that complaining, worrying, and stressing oneself are not solutions to problems but instead, a waste of time and energy. The message conveyed is that a positive and creative approach to life's challenges can lead to more effective outcomes.

Translation

Every night, Joha used to have a good time sitting and talking with his friends as they relaxed after a long day of work. However, Joha's friends kept complaining about the same problems and hardships they faced until he became bored hearing them complain. He tried to think of a solution and came up with an idea.

The next night when they met, Joha told his friends a funny story, and they all laughed. The next night, he told them the same funny story, but only a few of them laughed. Then again on the third night, he told them the same story, but this time, none of them laughed.

Joha smiled and asked, "Why did you not laugh at the story?"

His friends explained that it was because he was repeating the same story. Joha responded, "You did not laugh at the funny story more than once, so why do you keep complaining and whining about the same problems every time we meet? Think of a solution or talk about something else!"

كان جحا و أصحابه يجلسون معا في كل ليلة و يتحدثون. كانوا يريدون أن يقضوا وقتا ممتعا و يرتاحوا من مشقة العمل. لاحظ جحا أن أصحابه كانوا يتكلمون عن نفس المشاكل و المصاعب التي تواجههم في أعمالهم و حياتهم كل ليلة حتى سئم منهم و أصبح الجلوس معهم مزعجا. فكر جحا كثيرا و أخيرا وجد حلاً لهذا الموضوع.

وفي الليله التالية حين اجتمع الأصدقاء قال لهم جحا قصة مضحكة فضحكوا جميعا ، و في الليلة التي بعدها قال لهم نفس القصة المضحكة مرة أخرى فلم يضحكوا جميعا و لكن ابتسم عدد قليل منهم ، ثم في الليلة الثالثة قص عليهم نفس القصة و في هذه المرة لم يضحك أي واحد منهم

و عندئذ ابتسم جحا و قال لهم: لماذا لم تضحكوا على القصة؟ قالوا: لأنك قلتها لنا أكثر من مرة فقال لهم: القصة المضحكة لم تعجبكم و لم تضحكوا عليها أكثر من مرة فلماذا تستمرون في الشكوى و والتذمر على نفس المشاكل في كل ليلة؟ فكروا في حل أو تحدثوا عن موضوع مختلف

Vocabulary

Meaning	Plural	Word
Friend	أصحاب	صاحب
Night	ليال	ليلة
Noticed		لاحظ
Relax		يرتاح
Hardship	مشقات	مشقة
Problem	مشاكل	مشكلة
Difficulty	مصاعب	صعوبة
Laugh		ضحك
Another		أخرى
Got tired of something		سئم

Meaning	Plural	Word
Complain		تذمر
Many		كثيرا
Solution	حلول	حل
Job	أعمال	عمل
Annoying		مزعجا
Story	قصص	قصة
Then		ثم
Smiled		ابتسم
At this time		عندئذ

المناقشة:

1. ماذا كان يعمل جحا كل ليلة ؟

2. لماذا سئم جحا من أصحابة؟

3. ما رأيك في حل جحا لمشكلة أصحابة؟

القاضي جحا
Joha the Judge

Cultural Note

Joha is portrayed as a clever and intelligent character, which made people go to him to solve their problems or use him as a judge. He is known for his wit and his ability to use his unique means to solve problems in a creative and distinctive manner. He is often depicted as being able to outsmart those around him and solve the most difficult of situations.

When Joha was a judge, two men went to him to ask for his ruling. The first man said, "Your Honor, as I was walking and carrying a loaf of bread, I passed by this man's shop as he was grilling meat. Because I had no money to buy any meat, I cut pieces of my bread and passed them over the grill so that they would absorb some of the meat's aroma. When I started to go home, the owner of the shop grabbed me and asked me to pay for the smell. Is this acceptable? Should anyone have to pay for only the smell of food?"

Joha said to the owner of the shop, "How much do you want for the scent?"

The shopkeeper said, "Five dirhams, sir."

Joha looked at the owner of the loaf and said, "Take out five dirhams and throw them on the ground one by one." The man was surprised, but he threw his dirhams one after the other on the floor, and they all made a ringing sound.

Joha said to the owner of the barbeque, "Did you hear that ringing sound?" He replied, "Yes, sir, I heard it."

Joha said, "That ringing is the price of the smell. He ate with his nose, and now you got paid with your ear."

عندما كان جحا قاضياً جاء عنده رجلان و طلبا منه أن يحكم بينهم . فسألهم عن قصتهم . قال احدهما : كنت أمشي في طريقي و معي رغيفاً من الخبز فمررت بدكان هذا الرجل وكان يشوي لحماً فأعجبتني رائحة الشواء فبدأت أقطع الرغيف الى قطع صغيرة و أمرر كل قطعة فوق قطع اللحم و آكلة لأني ليس معي مال لأشتري اللحم . و حين انتهيت من أكل الرغيف أردت أن أذهب الى بيتي لكن أمسكني صاحب اللحم و طلب مني أن أدفع ثمن رائحة اللحم. هل هناك أحد يدفع ثمن رائحة الطعام ؟

نظر جحا الى صاحب الدكان و فكر قليلا ثم سأل صاحب الدكان : ما هو ثمن اللحم المشوي ؟ قال صاحب الدكان: خمسة دراهم أيها القاضي .

نظر جحا الى صاحب الرغيف و قال له : أخرج خمسة دراهم من جيبك و ارميها على الارض نظر الرجل الى القاضي مستغربا و أخرج الدراهم و رماها على الأرض واحدا بعد الاخر و كان كل درهم يرمية على الأرض يُخرج رنيناً.

سأل جحا صاحب الدكان: هل سمعت ذلك الرنين ؟ قال: نعم ياسيدي. سمعته

فقال له جحا : ذلك الرنين ثمن تلك الرائحة . لقد أكل بأنفه وها أنت قد أخذت أجرك بأذنك ثم أمر الرجل أن يأخذ دراهمه و ينصرف .

Vocabulary

Meaning	Plural	Word
Judge	قضاه	قاضي
Their story		قصتهم
Loaf	أرغفة	رغيفاً
Store	دكاكين	دكان
Barbequing		يشوي
Meat		لحم
I liked		أعجبتني
Smell	روائح	رائحة
Cut a piece		أقتطع

Meaning	Plural	Word
Pass it		أ مرر
Price		ثمن
Ringing		رنين
Money		مال
Buy		أشتري
Held me		أمسكني
Pay		أدفع
Leave		ينصرف

المناقشة:

1. ماذا فعل الرجل الأول ؟

2. لماذا طلب منه صاحب الشواء المال؟

3. كم كان ثمن الشواء؟

4. هل كان جحا قاضيا ذكيا؟

قصة نعل الملك
The King's Shoe

Cultural Note

The message of this story is that before attempting to change the world around you, it is important to focus on personal growth and development first. This may involve being more creative and resourceful in your approach to life's challenges. Improving oneself should be the first step in creating positive change. Additionally, it is important to have realistic expectations and not to expect others to perform miracles simply because they have been asked or you have the authority over them. This message encourages creativity and personal responsibility, reminding us that true change starts from within.

Translation

Once upon a time, there was a young king who ruled a huge country. One day, he decided to take a road trip to see his land and talk to his people. So in the morning, he set out walking in his bare feet.

He was enjoying his trip. However, on his way back to his palace, his feet became very swollen and painful from walking on the rough paths. When the king returned, he had an idea. The next morning, he met with his ministers and announced that he was going to issue a new law. To make traveling by foot easier, he ordered his workers to cover all the roads with leather. His ministers said this was impossible since they could not supply enough leather to cover all the roads. So they tried to come up with a new plan.

Finally one of the ministers suggested a simple solution. He explained that it would be much easier to take a small piece of leather and attach it to the bottom of each person's foot. This way, everyone could more comfortably walk on rough roads. The king liked the idea and ordered leather pieces to be produced in great numbers for everyone's feet.

This is how shoes were invented.

كان يا مكان في قديم الزمان كان هناك ملكا صغيرا في السن و كانت مملكته واسعة و كبيرة ، وفي يوم من الأيام اراد الملك أن يكتشف مملكته و يزور الاماكن التي فيها ويتعرف عليها . فخرج في الصباح و بدأ رحلته متنقلا من مكان الى آخر ماشيا على قدمية.

كان مستمتعا برحلته و لم يشعر بالتعب و لكن في طريق عودته الى القصر تورمت قدماه كثيرا بسبب المشي لمسافات طويلة في الطرق الوعرة التي يصعب السير فيها، وعندما عاد الملك الى القصر فكر كثيرا في حل لهذه المشكلة ، و في صباح اليوم التالي اجتمع مع وزرائه و قال لهم أنه يريد أن يصدر قرارا بتغطية جميع شوارع وطرق المملكة بالجلد، حتي لا تتأذي اقدامه و أقدام شعبة الذين يمشون في هذه الطرق الوعرة ، ولكن وزرائه قالوا أن هذا قرار صعب و لا يمكن أن نجد جلد يكفي لنغطي طرق المملكه كلها و لكن دعنا نفكر بحل أسهل.

و بدأوا يتناقشون و يفكرون في حل و أخيرا اقترح عليه أحد وزراء حلًا افضل و أسهل بكثير فقال: ما رأيك في أن نحضر قطعة صغيرة من الجلد و نضعها تحت قدمك و قدم كل من يريد أن يمشي في المملكه؟ أُعجب الملك بهذا الحل و أمر بصنع قطع جلدية توضع تحت الأقدام لمن يريد أن يمشي في الطرق الوعرة و كانت هذه بداية صنع الاحذية.

Vocabulary

Meaning	Plural	Word
King	ملوك	ملكا
Kingdom	ممالك	مملكة
Discover		يكتشف
Youth	شباب	شاب
Wide		واسعة
Rule		يحكم
Visit		يزور
Trip	رحلات	رحلة
Secret	أسرار	سر
Swollen		تورمت
Cover		تغطية

Meaning	Plural	Word
Rough path		الوعرة
Street	شوارع	شارع
Leather	جلود	جلد
Issued		أصدر
The case	قضايا	القضية
Minister	وزراء	وزير
Road	طرق	طريق
Harm		تتأذى
Foot	أقدام	قدم
People	شعوب	شعب
Let's		دعنا

المناقشة:

1. لماذا قام الملك بالرحلة داخل بلده؟

2. لماذا تورمت قدماه؟

3. ماذا قرر أن يعمل لحل هذه المشكلة؟

4. ماذا اقترح علية وزيره؟

كن قدوة حسنة
Be a Good Example

Cultural Note

Teaching good manners and values for children is an important aspect of parenting and is best done through setting a good example. Children are often more likely to learn and internalize good manners and values when they observe them being modeled by those around them, particularly their parents and caregivers. Rather than overwhelming children with a constant barrage of advice and teaching lessons, it is more effective to live by these values and principles in one's own behavior and actions. This story demonstrates the importance of setting a good example, which makes proper manners more meaningful to children, leading to the long-term internalization and implementation of these manners.

Translation

There once was a father who had two children: one was three years old and the second was seven years old. One day, the circus came to his city, so he took his two children. A sign on the ticket counter said: "Five dirhams for adults, three dirhams for those over six years old, and free for children under six years old."

The man ordered two tickets. He said, "One ticket for me and another ticket for my son, who is seven years old."

The ticket seller looked at him with a smile and said, "You are an honest person. You could have saved three dirhams by telling me that your son is under six, and I would not have known the difference."

The father replied, "Yes, you are right, but my children would know the difference. They know their ages, and they would know that I lied. If I lie, I will be a bad example for them for the rest of their lives. They would always remember that their father is a liar. Is this worth saving three dirhams?"

في يوم من الأيام كان هناك أب عنده ولدين . واحد منهما عمره ثلاث سنوات و الثاني عمره سبع سنوات . حين جاء السيرك الى المنطقة التي يعيش فيها الأب أخذ الأب طفليه إلى السيرك ليقضوا وقتا ممتعا معا . حين وصلوا الى السيرك كان مكتوبا على شُباك التذاكر: سعر التذكرة خمسة دراهم للبالغين وثلاثة دراهم لمن هم فوق ست سنوات ومجاناً لمن هم أقل من ست سنوات

قال الأب لقاطع التذاكر: أريد تذكرتين واحدة لشخص بالغ لي و واحدة لولدي وعمره سبع سنوات

ابتسم قاطع التذاكر و قال له: أنت شخص مميز . لو قلت لي أن ابنك أقل من ست فأنا لن أعرف الفرق و كنت وفرت على نفسك ثلاثة دراهم .

قال الأب: نعم كلامك صحيح و لكن أولادي يعرفون أعمارهم و سيعرفون أني كذبت و بذلك سأكون قدوة سيئة لهم طول حياتهم و سوف يتذكرون دائما أن أباهم كان يكذب و هم سيكذبون أيضا. هل هذا يستحق ثلاثة دراهم؟

Vocabulary

Meaning	Plural	Word
Child	أطفال	طفل
Year	سنوات	سنة
Boy	أولاد	ولد
Circus		سيرك
To spend		ليقضوا
Enjoyable		ممتعا
Mature	بالغين	بالغ
Free		مجانا
Price	أسعار	سعر
Together		معا
Written		مكتوبا

Meaning	Plural	Word
Ticket	تذاكر	تذكرة
Two tickets		تذكرتين
Save		توفر
Ticket seller		قاطع التذاكر
Know	يعرفون	يعرف
Example		قدوة
Deserve		يستحق
Less		أقل
Exceptional		مميز
Bad		سيئة

المناقشة:

1. الى أين ذهب الأب مع أولاده؟

2. كم كان سعر التذاكر؟

3. كم عمر أولاده ؟

4. هل هذا الأب قدوه حسنه؟

بيت للبيع
Home for Sale

Cultural Note

A common sentiment in Arabic culture is based on the concept of gratitude and appreciation for the blessings in one's life. The idea is that focusing on what we have, rather than what we lack, can help to cultivate a sense of contentment and satisfaction. Additionally, being grateful for what we have is believed to bring more blessings and abundance into one's life.

There is a verse in the Quran that Arabs keep repeating and reminding others about. It says, "If you thank Allah, God, for what you have, He will give you more." We always forget all the good things we have and concentrate on what we do not have. It is the same as when we complain because God made thorns under the roses instead of thanking Him for creating the roses.

The message is that by cultivating a spirit of gratitude and being thankful for what we have, we can create a more positive and fulfilling life for ourselves.

Translation

A man wanted to sell his house and move to another one as he felt that his house is old and wanted a bigger house in a better area. He has a friend who is a businessman and expert in marketing. The man went to his friend and talked to him about what he wants.

His friend said, "yes I will help you but first we have to put an advertisement to post in the newspaper." His friend knew the house well because he had visited many times, so he wrote a detailed description. He praised its beautiful location and large size, described its wonderful design, and talked about its big garden and its many different trees. Later, he went to his friend and read him the advertisement. His friend listened to him very carefully.

His friend asked him to read the ad again, which he did.

The homeowner shouted with excitement, "What a fantastic house! I have been dreaming all my life to live in such a wonderful house. I did not know that it was so great until I heard your description." Then he smiled and said, "Please do not post the ad. My house is not for sale anymore."

كان هناك رجل يريد أن يبيع بيته وينتقل إلى بيت آخر لأنه كان يشعر أن بيته قديم و هو يريد بيتا أكبر و في موقع أفضل. كان أحد أصدقاءه رجل أعمال و عنده خبرة في مجال التسويق. فذهب الية و جلس يحدثه عما يريد . قال له صديقه نعم سأساعدك. أولا يجب أن نضع اعلانا في الجريدة . وافق الرجل وطلب منه أن يساعده في كتابة اعلان لبيع البيت، وكان صديقه يزوره كثيرا و يعرف البيت جيدا فوافق

بعد عدة أيام أحضر الصديق الاعلان و كتب فيه وصفًا دقيقا للبيت و وصف فيه موقعه الجميل و أنه يقع في منطقة خضراء واسعة ومساحتة كبيرة ووصف التصميم الهندسي الرائع، ثم تحدث عن الحديقة التي حول البيت وعن أنواع الأشجار التي فيها ثم قرأ الإعلان على صاحب البيت الذي كان يستمع اليه باهتمام شديد.

قال الرجل لصديقه: : أرجوك اقرأ الإعلان مرة أخرى فأعاد صديقه القراءة.

صاح الرجل : هذا بيت رائع و كنت أحلم أن انتقل الى مثل هذا البيت، ولم أكن أدرك أن بيتي بهذا الجمال الا الآن بعد أن سمعتك تقرأ الاعلان ثم ابتسم وقال: من فضلك لا تنشر الإعلان فبيتي ليس للبيع . أريد أن أبقى في هذا البيت الجميل .

Vocabulary

Meaning	plural	word
To sell		يبيع
Better		أفضل
Newspaper		الجريدة
Move		ينتقل
Businessman	رجال أعمال	رجل أعمال
Expert	خبراء	خبير
Marketing		تسويق
To help him		يساعد
Advertisement	اعلانات	إعلان
Engineering design	تصميمات هندسية	تصميم هندسي
Attention	اهتمامات	اهتمام
Advertise		تنشر
Visit		يزور
Know		يعرف
Location	مواقع	موقع
Garden	حدائق	حديقة
Green		خضراء
Tree	أشجار	شجرة

المناقشة:

1. لماذا أراد الرجل أن يبيع بيته ؟

2. من الدي كتب الاعلان لبيع البيت ؟

3. كيف كان وصف البيت ؟

4. لماذا غير الرجل رأيه في بيع بيته؟

ثق بنفسك
Trust Yourself

Cultural Note

In the Arab world, people often form close friendships at a young age. Childhood friends often maintain their close relationships well into adulthood. These relationships can be based on shared interests, school, or family connections. Friends are often considered as close family members.

Friendship in the Arab world can take on a variety of forms, from close, personal relationships to more formal ones. However, regardless of the nature of the relationship, friends are expected to be there for each other in good and bad times, offering support, encouragement, and a shoulder to cry on. This sense of community is a key part of Arab culture and provides a sense of security and comfort. The close bonds between friends play a significant role in social and personal relationships.

However, keep in mind that not all the time, a friend's opinions are appropriate or suitable. Therefore, it is important to think and decide after consulting with others.

Trusting oneself is an important aspect of personal growth and self-confidence. It means having faith in your own abilities, decisions, instincts, and relying on yourself to make the right choices in life. When you trust yourself, you are more likely to take risks, pursue your passions, and face challenges with courage and determination.

This story explains that building trust in oneself takes time and effort. It requires facing and overcoming fears while developing a sense of inner strength. It also means being honest with yourself about your strengths and weaknesses and embracing both with self-compassion.

Translation

A group of frogs were traveling through the forest looking for food. Suddenly, three of them fell into a deep hole. The first frog looked up and, after realizing how deep the hole was, said to the other two, "This is a very deep hole and we cannot escape, so we shouldn't try to get out. Let's just stay here and wait to die." It did not try to jump or anything.

At first, the other two continued to try to escape. However, after a while, the second frog, who was the strongest of the three, started to get tired. He said, "I am very tired and we will not get out. I will stay here with the other frog and we will die together."

But the third frog continued to jump with all its strength in hopes of escaping the hole. The other frogs were watching from above and said, "Stop trying to escape! The hole is too deep. You won't be able to get out. Just give up."

كانت هناك مجموعة ضفادع تمشي في الغابة تبحث عن الطعام و الماء . وفجأة سقطت أول ثلاث ضفادع و التي كانت تمشي في المقدمة في حفرة عميقة . الضفدع الأول نظر الى أعلى و علم أن الحفرة عميقة فقال لهم لن نستطيع الخروج من هنا . لا داعي للمحاولة و استسلم و لم يحاول الخروج .

في البداية استمر الضفدعان في المحاولة و لكن مع مرور بعض الوقت، شعر الضفدع الثاني بالتعب رغم انه كان الأقوى بين جميع الضفادع و قرر أن يستسلم فنزل الى أسفل الحفرة و قال لقد تعبت و لن نستطيع الخروج سأبقى هنا مع الضفدع الآخر و سننتظر الموت هنا معا.

الضفدع الثالث لم يستسلم و على الرغم من انه كان ضعيفا لكنه كلما نظر الى الأعلى يرى الضفادع الأخرى تتحدث معه كان يظن أنهم يشجعونه و يريدونه أن يستمر في المحاولة. كانت الضفادع تقول لة : توقف ! الحفرة عميقة و لن تستطيع أن تخرج منها . و لكنه كان يتشجع ويقفز بقوة أكبر الى الأعلى و في النهاية خرج من الحفرة.

The third frog was weak, but it did not give up and it kept trying to escape. Whenever it saw the frogs at the top talking and pointing, it thought they were encouraging and it tried harder and harder until finally, it got out.

As the frogs congratulated the survivor, they were surprised to learn that it was deaf. The reason it escaped was that it thought that they were encouraging it to try harder instead of destroying its determination.

الضفدعة الثالثة لم تستسلم و كانت ضعيفة ، لكنها كانت تنظر للأعلى و ترى الضفادع الأخرى تتحدث معها كانت تظن أنهم يشجعونها و يريدونها أن تستمر في المحاولة فكانت تتشجع وتقفز بقوة أكبر الى الأعلى و في النهاية خرجت من الحفرة.

بدأت الضفادع تتحدث مع الضفدعة الثالثة التي خرجت من الحفرة و لكن تفاجأ الجميع بأنها صمّاء لا تسمع ولا تتكلم و كان سبب نجاحها و خروجها من الحفرة أنها ظنت أن الضفادع كانت تشجعها على الخروج بينما في الواقع كانوا يهدمون من عزيمتها

Vocabulary

Meaning	Plural	Word
Frog	ضفادع	ضفدع
The rest		باقي
Impossible		مستحيل
Hole	حفر	حفرة
Jumped		قفز
Died		مات
Submit		استسلم
Weak	ضعفاء	ضعيف
Trying		يحاول

Meaning	Plural	Word
Deaf		أصم
Encourage		يشجع
Forest	غابات	غابة
Suddenly		فجأة
Deep		عميقة
Beginning		مقدمة
Top		أعلى
Trial	محاولات	محاولة
Hope	آمال	أمل

المناقشة:

1. ماذا كانت تفعل الضفادع ؟

2. أين سقطت ثلاث ضفادع؟

3. ماذا فعل الضفدع الأول ؟

4. ماذا فعل الضفدع الثاني ؟

5. لماذا لم يستسلم الضفدع الثالث ؟

هذا حال الدنيا
This is Life

Cultural Note

It is important to thank Allah for everything that we have, whether we believe it is good or bad. In Arab culture, when people greet each other, the first question they ask is, "How are you?" And the response always starts with, "*Alhamdulilla*, thank God, we are OK." Only then is it appropriate to complain to close friends or family members about how tough or hard life is.

This story describes that people are not the same—what is good for you might not be good for your friend or next-door neighbor. Everyone has their own situation. What is good for you might be a problem for others, so always be thankful to God. It is also very common for children to ask their parents to make **dua** (pray) for them, so Allah will protect them.

Translation

There once was a man who had two daughters. The first was married to a farmer who had a large farm. The second was married to the owner of a pottery factory. After a while, the man wanted to visit his daughters to make sure they were OK. So, he told his wife, got ready, and left.

He first went to his daughter who was the farmer's wife. She welcomed him with joy and was very happy to see him. When he asked how they were, the daughter said, "*Alhamdulillah*, praise be to God, we are fine. My husband borrowed money, bought seeds, and planted them. We are praying that it will rain and our seeds will grow. That way, we will have many fruits and vegetables to sell. If it rains, we will have a good business. However, if it does not rain, then this will be a great misfortune. Please pray for us to have rain!"

في يوم من الأيام كان هناك رجل عنده بنتين . تزوجت الأولى من رجل فلاح و كان عنده مزرعة كبيرة. وتزوجت الثانية من رجل عندة مصنع فخار . بعد فترة من الزمن أراد الرجل أن يطمئن على بناته و أخبر زوجته أنه سيسافر ليرى بناته و يطمئن عليهما .

و بعد أن أستعد الرجل سافر ليزور ابنتيه . في البداية ذهب عند إبنته زوجة الفلاح . استقبلته ابنته و زوجها بفرح و كانوا سعداء جدا بزيارته . وعندما سأل عن أحوالهم قالوا له : الحمد لله نحن بخير و لكن الزوج استدان بعض المال ليشتري البذور و قد زرعها في أرضه . و اننا ندعوا أن تمطر الدنيا حتى ينمو الزرع و تنبت الخضار و الفواكه و نبيعها و بذلك لا نحتاج أحدا و نكون بخير وإن لم تمطر فإننا سنفقد كل شيئ و ستكون أحوالنا سيئة . أدع لنا يا أبي أن تمطر الدنيا!

The next day, he went to visit his second daughter who was the wife of the pottery factory owner. They greeted him with great joy and pleasure. And when he asked about how they were, his daughter said, "*Alhamdulillah*, praise be to God, we are fine. My husband borrowed money, bought materials, and worked very hard to create his pottery. He left it under the sun to dry. We are praying that we will not have any rain until it dries to be able to sell the pottery and make money. If it rains, then we will lose everything because the pottery will be ruined and there will be a great calamity. Please pray for us that it will not rain!"

The man returned home and his wife asked him how their daughters were doing. He explained the situation to her and told her, "If it rains, be thankful, and if it does not rain, be thankful, too!"

وفي اليوم التالي ذهب الرجل لزيارة ابنته الثانية زوجة صاحب مصنع الفخار التي استقبلته هي و زوجها بفرح كبير أيضا . و عندما سأل عن أحوالهم قالت البنت: الحمدلله نحن بخير و قد استدان زوجي مالا و اشترى التراب و عمل عليه كثيرا وحوله إلى فخار و قد وضعه تحت الشمس حتى يجف . اننا ندعوا أن لا تمطر الدنيا حتى يجف الفخار و نبيعه و نكسب مالا كثيرا و لكن ان أمطرت الدنيا فاننا سنخسر كل شيئ لان الفخار سيذوب و ستكون هناك مصيبة كبيرة ادع لنا يا أبي أن لا تمطر الدنيا حتى تكون أحوالنا بخير .

ولما عاد الرجل إلى زوجته سألته عن بناتها فشرح لها ما حدث و قال لها إن أمطرت فاحمدي الله و إن لم تمطر فاحمدي الله

Vocabulary

Meaning	Plural	Word
Get married		تزوج
Farmer	فلاحين	فلاح
Farm	مزارع	مزرعة
Factory	مصانع	مصنع
Pottery		فخار
Get a debt		استدان
Happiness	أفراح	فرح
Disaster	مصائب	مصيبة
Happy	سعداء	سعيد

Meaning	Plural	Word
Thank		حمد
Seed	بذور	بذرة
Rain	أمطار	مطر
Will lose		سنفقد
Travel		يسافر
Land	أراض	أرض
We Pray		ندعوا
Too		أيضاً

لمناقشة:

1. لمن زوّج الرجل ابنته الأولى ؟

2. ماذا يعمل زوج ابنته الثانية؟

3. ماذا طلبت منه ابنته الأولى ؟

4. ماذا طلبت منه ابنته الثانية؟

5. لو كنت أنت مكان هذا الأب ماذا ستفعل ؟

كما تدين تُدان
As You Condemn, You Will be Condemned

Cultural Note

In Arabic culture, parents are responsible for their children. They pay for all their needs until they get married. It is very rare to see children leaving their parents' house before they get married. When parents get very old and cannot support themselves, then it is usually the oldest son's responsibility to take care of his parents and support them. The other sons and daughters would communicate and help with monetary payments, cleaning, buying food, and providing for all their needs.

There is a popular saying in the Arab world: "As you condemn, you will be condemned." Sometimes, it is used to encourage children to take care of their parents, as in this story. Other times, it is used to encourage everyone to be good and treat others as you wish to be treated. This cultural value emphasizes the importance of family and respect for elders, as well as the idea of reciprocity and treating others as one would like to be treated.

Translation

There once was a man who lived with his wife and young son. When his mother passed away, his father came to live with him. His wife did not like the idea. After a while, she started to complain about him. She told her husband that his father embarrassed her in front of her friends because he is so forgetful that he keeps repeating the same story. After a while, the husband became fed up with his wife's resentment, her complaints about his father, and the embarrassment he was causing her. So he decided to get rid of his father by sending him to a nursing home.

The husband started to collect his father's things. However, he was worried about him because he was not sure if he would be treated well at the nursing home. As he continued packing, he ignored the fact of how well his father took care of him as a child and all the sacrifices he made. After he was done, he put all his father's belongings and some food into a bag. He also gave his father a large piece of sponge to use as a mattress to sleep on.

كان هناك رجل و زوجته و بعد أن توفت والدته أخذ أبيه ليعيش عنده في بيته . لكن الزوجة لم يعجبها ذلك ومع الوقت بدأت تشتكي من أبيه و تتذمر منه و كانت تقول أنه يحرجها بتصرفاته و ذاكرته الضعيفة أمام صديقاتها و أنه كان يكرر نفس القصة مرات عديدة كل يوم و مع مرور الوقت و كثرة الشكوي من زوجته قرر الرجل التخلص من أبيه المسن و وضعه في بيت لرعاية المسنين.

بدأ الرجل يجمع حاجيات أبيه و كان متأثرا جدا و قلقا عليه و هو يفكر هل سيعاملة الناس في دار الرعاية معاملة حسنة و هل سيلبون احتياجاته و مع ذلك استمر في جمع ملابس أبيه و نسى كل ما ضحى به أبوه لأجله و كيف أنه قدم له كل ما كان يحتاجه حين كان في بيت أبيه . لكنّ زوجته و إلحاحها الدائم كان الدافع لتصرفه . جمع الرجل بعض الطعام والملابس و وضعها في حقيبة، ثم حمل معه قطعة كبيرة من الإسفنج لينام عليها والده هناك في دار رعاية المسنين .

The man held his father's hand on his way to the door. On his way out, the man's young son asked his grandfather to leave the sponge. The man was very surprised and asked his son, "What do you want with this sponge? It is now my father's bed!"

The child innocently replied: "I want to save it for you so you will have something to sleep on when you get old and I take you to the nursing home, dad!"

The man stood speechless at what he heard from his little child. He cried with tears that wet his beard. He recalled all the things his father had done for him in his childhood and everything he had given him. The man then threw the bag on the ground, hugged his father for a long time, and pledged before God and his young son to take care of him himself as long as he was alive.

أمسك الرجل بيد أبيه متوجهاً إلى باب المنزل و لكن ابنه الصغير أمسك به و كان يطلب من أبيه بالحاح أن يترك له نصف قطعة الاسفنج التي يحملها معه . أستغرب الرجل من طلب ابنه و توقف لسؤاله : ماذا تريد بهذه القطعة من الاسفنج ؟ انه فراش أبي!

نظر اليه الطفل و قال ببراءة: أريد أن أحتفظ به لك حين آخذك الى دار الرعاية عندما تكبر في السن و تأتي لتسكن في بيتي !

توقف الرجل مصدوما مما قاله ابنه الصغير ، و بدأ يبكي حتى ابتلت لحيته من كثرة بكائه ، تذكر كل ما عمله أبوه لأجله في طفولته و كيف كان يساعده في كل شيئ في حياته ثم رمى ما كان يحمله على الأرض و عانق أباه عناقاً طويلاً و وعده برعايته بنفسه ما دام على قيد الحياة.

Vocabulary

Meaning	Plural	Word
Taking care of		رعاية
Get rid of		التخلص
Elder	مسنين	مسن
Discontent		استياء
Became very tired		ضاق ذرعاً
Embarrassment		حرج
Insistence		إلحاح
Sponge		الإسفنج
Save it		أبقيه
Shocked		مصدوما
Mattress		فراش
Cry		يبكي
Beard		لحية
Remember		تذكر
As long as		ما دام
Life		الحياة

المناقشة:

1. لماذا قرر الرجل أن يأخذ أبيه الى دار المسنين؟

2. ماذا أخذ معة ؟

3. ماذا كان بريد ابنه الصغير ؟ لماذا؟

4. ما رأيك في نهاية القصة؟

ساعد المحتاج
Relieve the Anxious

Cultural Note

In Arabic culture, people are supposed to help the needy and support them. Many people give money to help the less fortunate. There are many poor, starving, and destitute people everywhere, and not only in Arab countries. Arabs believe that giving charity is crucial for both sides, the needy and the wealthy. It helps the needy and supports their needs while it brings comfort and happiness to the rich. It is encouraged all the time, even when people are not that rich, because Arabs believe that if you help someone today, then God will help you and send someone to help you whenever you need any kind of help. There are many stories that are shared to enforce this habit. Helping the needy is a way to show compassion and fulfill one's moral obligations.

Translation

A famous circus once went to perform in a small village in the countryside. Most of the villagers took their children to see the circus and many people were standing in line to buy their tickets. Among those in line was a farmer whose appearance indicated that he was poor. He was waiting for his turn with his wife and four children, who were very joyful and excited for this happy occasion.

When it was the farmer's turn at the ticket center, he asked for tickets for himself and his family. But when the saleswoman told him the price of the tickets, he looked at her in shock. The price of the tickets was much more than he expected, and he did not have enough money. He grabbed the money in his pocket and started counting it, then sweat began to pour from his forehead. His wife lowered her head, not knowing what to do, and his children began to look at him with surprise and wondered "why wasn't he paying for the tickets?"

The man standing behind him noticed what was happening, and although he wasn't rich, he wanted to help the farmer. He took out some money from his pocket and threw down next to the farmer's leg and said to him, "This money fell from you onto the ground," and he bent down, picked up the money, and gave it to the farmer.

The farmer looked at the man with a look of thanks and gratitude and with tears falling down his cheek said to him, "Thank you very much, sir! I will never forget what you did for the rest of my life!"

في يوم من الأيام ذهب سيرك مشهور ليعمل عرض في قرية صغيرة في الريف . أسرع معظم سكان القرية و أخذوا أطفالهم ليشاهدوا السيرك فقد كانت هذه مناسبة سعيدة و لا تحدث كثيرا . وكان هناك صفا طويلا يقف أمام شباك التذاكر. كان من بين الواقفين مزارع يدل مظهره على أنه فقير و كان ينتظر دوره مع زوجته و أطفاله الأربعة الذين كانوا سعداء جدا و فرحين بهذه المناسبة

و حين جاء دور المزارع على شباك التذاكر طلب ست تذاكر له و لعائلته. و لكن حين قالت له البائعة ثمن التذاكر نظر اليها و هو مصدوم فقد كان ثمن التذاكر أكثر كثيرا مما توقعه و لم يكن معه المال الكافي .و بقي واقفا يفكر و لا يدري ماذا يفعل .أمسك النقود التي في جيبه و بدأ يعدها ثم بدأ العرق يتصبب من جبينه و خفضت زوجته وجهها لا تدري كيف تتصرف و بدأ أولاده ينظرون اليه باستغراب و يفكرون: لماذا لا يدفع ثمن التذاكر؟

لاحظ الرجل الذي كان يقف خلفه ما يحدث و على الرغم من أنه هو أيضا لا يبدو عليه الغنى الا أنه أراد أن يساعد المزارع و أخرج من جيبه بعض النقود و رماها بجانب رِجل المزارع ثم قال له: لقد وقعت هذه النقود منك على الأرض و انحنى ليأخذ النقود و أعطاها للمزارع.

نظر المزارع إلى الرجل نظرة شكر و امتنان و الدمعة تسقط على خده و قال له: شكرا جزيلا يا سيدي! لن أنسى لك ما فعلت طول حياتي !

Vocabulary

Meaning	Plural	Word
Countryside	أرياف	ريف
Show	عروض	عرض
Line	صفوف	صف
Ticket	تذاكر	تذكرة
Farmer	مزارعين	مزارع
Eagerness		شوق
Happiness	أفراح	فرح
Occasion	مناسبات	مناسبة
Salesperson	بائعين ـ بائعات	بائع – بائعة
Sweat		عرق
Wondering	تساؤلات	تساؤل
Secretly		خفية
Questioning		استغراب
Gratitude		امتنان

المناقشة:

1. من ذهب الى القرية؟

2. كم تذكرة يحتاج المزارع للدخول الى السيرك؟

3. هل كان معه مبلغ كاف من المال؟

4. من ساعدة ؟

حسِن الظن
Assume Good Intentions

Cultural Note

Family visits and gatherings are very important to Arabic families. Arabs place a strong emphasis on the importance of maintaining close family ties and visiting family members regularly. Arabs believe that their obligation toward their family is more important than their obligations to their work, friends, and even personal needs.

Hosting visitors is seen as a way of showing hospitality, respect, and generosity. The host welcomes the visitors at the door and invites them in with a smile, and the visitor greets everyone in the house by shaking hands, hugging, and kissing them on the cheeks, starting with the person on their right side. Men kiss their male relatives and friends and women kiss and hug female relatives and friends. Close family members—men and women—sit together. Usually, the host will present tea, coffee, sweets, nuts, and food.

The proximity of family members during visits, regardless of gender, reflects the close-knit nature of Arab families and the importance placed on maintaining strong family bonds.

Translation

There once was a man who had one daughter and went to visit her every week with his wife. After a while, he noticed that his son-in-law was annoyed whenever they came. The daughter's actions suggested that she and her husband were not happy with her parents' visits, but she and her husband did not want to tell them about it openly.

The man talked to his wife and she said that she also noticed this. The man agreed with his wife that they should invite their daughter and her husband to visit them instead. They felt that they were very happy with the invitation and they made it a weekly visit every Friday.

A few months later, the daughter's husband asked, "When will you come to visit us at our house?"

The father replied: "It is not important where we meet. What is important is to see each other and see how you are doing." The daughter's husband insisted that they would meet at their home next Friday.

كان هناك رجل عنده بنت واحدة متزوجة و كان يذهب لزيارتها كل أسبوع مع زوجته . بعد فترة من الوقت لاحظ هذا الرجل أن زوج إبنته يتضايق كلما ذهبوا لزيارته و كذلك كانت تصرفات ابنته توحي أنهم غير مرتاحين بزيارتهم و لكنهم لا يريدون أن يتحدثوا معهم في هذا الموضوع بصراحة .

تحدث الرجل مع زوجته و سألها ان كانت لاحظت ما لاحظه و قالت له أنها هي أيضا لاحظت ذلك . اتفق الرجل مع زوجته على أن يدعوا ابنتهم و زوجها لزيارتهم . و شعروا ان ابنتهم و زوجها يفرحون كثيرا بهذه الدعوة و جعلوها عادة أسبوعية في كل يوم جمعة .

بعد مرور عدة أشهر سأل زوج البنت : متى ستأتون لزيارتنا في بيتنا ؟ فقال له الأب: ليس المهم أين نتقابل و لكن المهم أن نراكم و نطمئن عليكم . أصر زوج البنت أن يكون اللقاء في بيتهم يوم الجمعة المقبل

When they went to visit, their son-in-law said to them, "We have visited you a lot, but from now on, every Friday you will come to visit us here in our house. And I want to tell you something. I had borrowed some money, and the owner of the debt began to demand repayment and told me he would come to my house to take my debt. I was afraid that he would come at any moment while you were here because I was late with my payments. But now that I have paid the debt, I am very happy you are here. I was afraid that he would come in your presence, and you would lose respect for me."

The man said to his son-in-law, "You have wronged us, and we have wronged you. If you had told me about your debt, I would have paid it for you. Instead, we misunderstood and thought that you did not want us to visit so please forgive us. We do not always see what is in each other's hearts."

فذهبوا لزيارته فقال لهم زوج ابنتهم: لقد زرناكم كثيرا و لكن من الآن و في كل جمعة أنتم ستأتون لزيارتنا هنا في بيتنا . و أريد أن أخبركم شيئا بصراحة . كنت قد استدنت مبلغا من المال و بدأ صاحب الدين يطالب بماله و يقول لي سآتي الى بيتك لآخذ ديني ، وكنت أتوقع أن يأتي في أي لحظه و انتم في بيتي لأني تأخرت في السداد و قد كنت محرجا جدا أما الآن فقد سددت ديني و أنا سعيد بزيارتكم . فقد كنت أخاف أن يأتي الرجل الى بيتي و أنتم عندي و يطالبني بماله في وجودكم فأصبح قليلاً في نظركم

فقال له : ظلمتنا وظلمناك . لو أخبرتني عن دينك كنت سأدفعه عنك و لقد أسأنا الظن بك و اعتقدنا أنك لا تحب زيارتنا لكم فأرجو أن تسامحنا . أننا لا نرى ما في القلوب .

Vocabulary

Meaning	Plural	Word
Annoyed, bothered		يتضايق
Behavior	تصرفات	تصرف
Whenever		كلما
Gives the impression		توحي
Embarrassed		تتحرج
Repeated		متكررة
Honestly		بصراحة
Habit	عادات	عادة
Invitation	دعوات	دعوة
Friday		جمعة
Insisted		صمم

Meaning	Plural	Word
Month	أشهر	شهر
Debt	ديون	دين
Doubt	شكوك	شك
I borrowed		استدنت
Asking for		يطالب
Late		تأخر
Injustice		ظلم
Forgive		يسامح
Pay		يدفع
Doubt		الظن

المناقشة:

1. ماذا لاحظ الأب ؟

2. هل لاحظت الأم ما لاحظه زوجها ؟

3. ماذا قرر الأب و الأم ؟

4. لماذا كان زوج البنت غير مرتاح لزيارة أهل زوجته؟

أحب كل الناس
Love All People

Cultural Note

The role of teachers goes beyond just imparting academic knowledge. They play an important role in shaping the character and values of students. A good teacher not only teaches the subject matter, but also instills in students a love for learning, help in developing critical thinking skills, and a positive attitude toward life. By providing emotional support, mentorship, and guidance, teachers have a lasting impact on the lives of their students. The bond between teacher and student can be truly special, and it is rewarding to see students grow and succeed, both academically and personally.

I still remember my math teacher in high school and how supportive and helpful she was. As a teacher myself, I feel very proud when my students show happiness to see me after 10 or more years and they come to talk and tell me their achievements.

How beautiful it is to live this short life with love and forgiveness for others and by accepting them as they are.

Translation

Once, at a school, a teacher told her students that they were going to play a game. She asked them to bring a bag with a bunch of potatoes. She asked them to write the name of someone they hated on each potato. The next day, each child brought a bag of potatoes with the names of the people they hated written on them. Some students had one potato, some two, some three, others five, and so on. Then, the teacher told them the one rule of the game was that they would have to carry the bag of potatoes with them wherever they went for one week.

After three days, the students began to grow tired of carrying the bag as well as the bad odor coming from the bags. When they told the teacher, she said they had to accept the smell and the weight of the bag for the few remaining days. Of course, the more potatoes, the heavier the bag and the stronger the smell.

في يوم من أيام الصيف و في احدى المدارس طلبت معلمة من طلابها في الفصل أن يحضروا معهم كيس فيه عدد من حبات البطاطا و أن يكتب كل طالب على كل حبة بطاطا اسم شخص يكرهه و قالت لهم أنهم سيلعبون لعبة معا . وفي اليوم التالي أحضر كل طالب كيس فيه بطاطا و مكتوب على كل حبة اسم شخص يكرهونه. بعض الطلاب كان معهم حبة بطاطا واحدة ، و بعضهم حبتين و بعضهم ثلاث حبات وآخرين خمس حبات وهكذا . ثم قالت لهم المعلمة شرط اللعبة وهو أن يحمل كل طالب كيس البطاطا معه أينما ذهب لمدة أسبوع واحد فقط

بعد ثلاثة أيام بدأ الطلاب يشعرون بالتعب و يشمون رائحة كريهة تخرج من كيس البطاطا و حين أخبروا المعلمة قالت لهم أن عليهم تحمّل الرائحة وثقل الكيس أيضا . بالطبع كلما زاد عدد حبات البطاطا كان الكيس أثقل و كانت الرائحة أقوى.

At the end of the week, the students were happy because the game was over. Then, the teacher asked them how they felt about carrying the bags of potatoes for a week. The children began to complain of fatigue and the difficulties that they felt carrying the smelly bag wherever they went.

The teacher then explained to them the goal of the game saying, "This is exactly what you will feel when you hate someone because hatred will pollute your heart, hold bad feelings inside, and you will think about it wherever you go. You have learned that you can't stand the smell of potatoes for a week but can you bear to hate anyone for the rest of your life? All you have to do is forgive others and do not keep thinking about their mistakes!"

في نهاية الأسبوع فرح الطلاب لأن اللعبة انتهت ثم سألتهم المعلمه عن احساسهم و هم يحملون كيس البطاطا لمدة أسبوع ، و بدأ الأطفال يشكون من التعب و الصعوبات التي شعروا بها و هم يحملون الكيس ذو الرائحة الكريهة أينما يذهبون . و بعد أن انتهوا من شرح الصعوبات التي واجهوها سألتهم المعلمة : أتعرفون ما هدف هذه اللعبة ؟ استغرب الطلاب و لم يعرفوا الاجابة

فقالت لهم : أردت أن أوضح لكم بالتطبيق العملي نتيجة الكراهية . احساسكم اليوم هو ما ستشعرون به بالضبط حين تكرهون شخصا و تحملون الكراهية في قلوبكم . الكراهية تلوث القلب وتجعل كل من يحملها يفكر بها دائما . هذه اللعبة علمتكم أنكم لا تستطيعون تحمل رائحة البطاطا لمدة أسبوع فهل بامكانكم تحمل الكراهية لاي شخص طول عمركم ؟ كل ما عليكم أن تفعلوه هو أن تسامحوا الآخرين و لا تفكروا في أخطائهم .

Vocabulary

Meaning	Plural	Word
Teacher (female)	معلمات	معلمة
Game	لُعَب	لُعبة
Student	طلاب	طالب
Fruit	حبات	حبة
Bag	أكياس	كيس
Potato		بطاطا
Week	أسابيع	أسبوع
Hate		يكره
Next		تالي
Foul		كريهة
Finished		انتهت
Complain	يشكون	يشكي

Meaning	Plural	Word
Significance		مغزى
Some		بعض
Others	آخرين / آخرون	آخر
And so on		و هكذا
Condition	شروط	شرط
Wherever		أينما
Foul		نتنة
Goal	أهداف	هدف
Will pollute		ستلوث
Persevere		تحمّل
Result	نتائج	نتائج

المناقشة:

١. ماذا طلبت المعلمة من الطلاب في الصف ؟

٢. ماذا كانت شروط اللعبة؟

٣. لماذا فرح الطلاب بأن اللعبة انتهت ؟

٤. ما هو هدف هذه اللعبة؟

فكر بعقل من حولك
Think with Their Minds

Cultural Note

Wearing jewelry made of gold is very common for women in the Arab world. Diamond jewelry is not very common. In the streets, you can see women walking around with their many gold bracelets, rings, and necklaces. Even women who are not rich can be seen wearing gold because it is part of their dowry or gifts for Eid, religious holidays, or special occasions. Additionally, gold is often passed down as heirlooms.

This story reflects this while at the same time, explaining that you can reach your goals by communicating with people and understanding their interests. This is a valuable lesson for both professional and personal relationships.

Translation

Once upon a time, a king noticed that the women who walked the streets in his kingdom wore a lot of jewelry, bragged about what they wore, and competed over who could wear the most. He believed this was a problem so he thought of a solution. He issued a decree banning women from wearing any gold, jewelry, and other adornments outside their houses. Of course, the women did not like this decision and they refused to follow the ruling. They began to complain and talk to everyone who had authority in the kingdom to overturn this decision. The city was pulsating with the sounds of protests, and women began to wear more and more gold and all kinds of jewelry.

The king did not like their reaction and was perplexed about what to do. So, he ordered an emergency meeting so he could consult with his ministers and those close to him. At the meeting, the king discussed his decision and the women's reaction, and then he asked for their opinion on the matter.

One of the ministers said, "I suggest reversing this decision to satisfy the women." Another said, "No, retracting the decision is proof that we are weak and afraid of them. We must be strong in front of the people so that they follow our orders." The advisers were divided into supporters and opponents of overturning the decision.

The king responded, "Wait a minute, and let us listen to our wisest adviser. What do you think? We did not hear your opinion!"

في قديم الزمان لاحظ أحد الملوك أن النساء تلبس الكثير من الحلى و الذهب في شوارع المملكة و تتفاخر بما تلبسة و يتسابقن من تلبس حلي أكثر . و كان ذلك يسبب الكثير من المشاكل للنساء و العائلات التي لا تستطيع أن تشتري الذهب و الحلي و أخذ يفكر في حل لهذ ا الموضوع . بعد عدة أيام أصدر قرارا يمنع فيه النساء من لبس الذهب والحلي خارج البيت . بالطبع هذا القرار لم يعجب النساء و كانت ردة الفعل كبيرة بينهن و رفضن اتباع هذا القرار لأنهن اعتدن على ذلك وبدأت النساء يتذمرن و يتحدثن مع كل من له سلطة في المملكة لايقاف هذا القرار وضجت المدينة بأصوات الإحتجاجات وبدأت النساء بالمبالغة بلبس الذهب و كل أنواع الحلى

ردة فعل النساء كانت قوية جدا و لم تعجب الملك و بدأ يفكر في حل آخر وإحتار ماذا يفعل . ثم قرر أن يستشير وزراءه و المقربين منه و أمر بعقد إجتماع طارئ معهم . ، فحضروا جميعا و أخبرهم الملك بقراره و بردة فعل النساء ثم طلب رأيهم في هذا الموضوع .

فقال أحدهم :أقترح التراجع عن هذا القرار حتى ترضى النساء و قال آخر : كلا إن التراجع و تغيير القرار دليل على أننا ضعفاء و نخاف منهم ويجب أن نكون أقوياء أمام الشعب حتى يتبعوا أوامرنا . وإنقسم المستشارون إلى مؤيد ومعارض

فقال الملك : انتظروا قليلا و دعونا نستمع الى حكيم المملكة . ما رأيك يا حكيم؟

The adviser said, "Oh king if you only think about what you want, the people will not listen to you. But if you reason with the people they will listen to you and obey."

The king said, "What do you think should be done? Shall we retract the decision?"

The adviser said, "No, but I suggest that you issue a decision clarifying that only beautiful women cannot wear jewelry because beautiful women do not need adornment, however, ugly women can wear any jewelry that they want because they need something that will make them beautiful."

The king liked the idea very much and issued the new decree the next day. After several hours, women began taking off their jewelry because they did not want to be seen as admitting they were ugly.

Then the wise adviser said, "People will obey you if you think with their minds and understand their thoughts."

قال الحكيم : أيها الملك أذا فكرت بما تريده أنت فلن يستمع الشعب لك . فكر بطريقة تجعل الناس يستمعون اليك و يطيعونك .

فقال الملك : في رأيك ما العمل ؟ هل نتراجع عن القرار؟

قال الحكيم : لا ولكن أقترح أن تصدر قرارا يوضح أن الجميلات فقط لا يمكنهن أن يلبس الذهب والحلى للزينه لأن الجميلات لسن بحاجة إلى الزينة و أما القبيحات فيمكنهن أن يلبسن ما يردن من الذهب و الحلي لأنهم بحاجة الى شيئ يظهر جمالهن.

أعجبت الفكره الملك كثيرا و أصدر القرار الجديد في اليوم التالي. و بعد مرور عدة ساعات بدأت النساء بخلع الحلي و الزينة لأن كل واحدة منهن اعتقدت أنها جميلة و لا تحتاج إلى أي زينة

عندئذ قال الحكيم : سيطيعك الناس اذا فكرت بعقولهم و أدركت إهتماماتهم

Vocabulary

Meaning	Plural	Word	Meaning	Plural	Word
Prohibit		يمنع	Kind	أنواع	نوع
Gold		الذهب	Emergency	طوارئ	طارئ
Woman	نساء	امرأة	Hold		عقد
Adornments		الحلي	Meeting	اجتماعات	اجتماع
Show off		تتفاخر	Opinion	آراء	رأي
Decision	قرارات	قرار	Topic	موضوعات	موضوع
Reaction	ردود فعل	ردة فعل	Retract		التراجع
Refused		رفضت	Accept		ترضى
Protest	احتجاجات	احتجاج	Weak	ضعفاء	ضعيف
Sign	مؤشرات	مؤشر	Scared		نخاف
Advisor	مستشارون	مستشار	Order	أوامر	أمر
Wise	حكماء	حكيم	Suggest		أقترح
Exception	استثناءات	إستثناءً	Ugly	قبيحات	قبيحة
Take off		خلع	Supporter	مؤيدون	مؤيد
Beauty		جمال	Opponent	معارضون	معارض

المناقشة:

1. ماذا كان قرار الملك؟

2. ماذا كانت ردة فعل النساء في البداية؟

3. ماذا كان رأي المستشارين ؟

4. ما هي نصيحه الحكيم؟

5. ما رأيك في نصيحة الحكيم ؟

زرقاء اليمامة
The Blue-Eyed Yamamah

Cultural Note

The Blue-Eyed Yamamah refers to a very beautiful Arab woman with blue eyes who was able to see things from very far distances. She used to live in an area called Yamamah in Saudi Arabia. "He sees better than the Blue-Eyed Yamamah" is a proverb used in the Arab world to praise someone's sharpness of vision, regardless of their physical appearance. The reference to the Blue-Eyed Yamamah is just a metaphor to describe the person's keen sight.

On a side note: There is a misconception that all Arabs have brown or dark skin with black or brown hair and eyes, which is not true. I am an Arab; my father had light-brown skin with black eyes, while my mom was very blonde with green eyes. This is a general fact that applies to many families. The Blue-Eyed Yamamah is another example reflecting that Arabs might be Black, brown, or very white. In other words, Arabs come in a variety of skin tones, hair colors, and eye colors, the same as any other culture or ethnicity.

Translation

There was once a very beautiful woman who lived in a place called Al-Yamamah, a region of Saudi Arabia. This woman had blue eyes and very strong eyesight and could see things from very far away. So, she was called "Blue Yamamah."

Zarqa Al-Yamamah lived with her populous tribe in Al-Yamamah. Many wars happened between her tribe and the tribes around them, and Zarqa Al-Yamamah helped her people in their wars because she would stand on the mountain, watch the enemies and their movements, and then she would tell her tribe how to prepare for the fight. Every time, she was the reason for her tribe's victory. In honor of her, boys and girls cheered and greeted her after all of the wars.

كان هناك امرأة جميله جدا تعيش في منطقة كبيرة اسمها اليمامة أحدى مناطق السعودية . و كانت هذه المرأة عيونها زرقاء و بصرها قوي جدا و تستطيع رؤية الأشياء من مسافة بعيدة جدا . لذلك سُميت هذه المرأة "زرقاء اليمامة"

كانت زرقاء اليمامة تعيش مع قبيلتها الكبيرة في اليمامة و كانت تحدث بين قبيلتها وبين القبائل التي حولها حروب عديدة ، وقد ساعدت زرقاء اليمامة قبيلتها في حروبهم، حيث كانت تقف على الجبل وترى الأعداء واتجاهاتهم، ثمّ تخبر قبيلتها كي يستعدّوا للقتال، وفي كلّ مرة كانت هي السبب في انتصار قبيلتها، وتكريماً لها كان كل أفراد القبيلة يهتفون لها ويُحيّونها بعد كل انتصار .

There was a king who wanted to attack the tribe of Zarqa al-Yamamah. One of his followers told him that there was a woman named Zarqa al-Yamamah, informed him about her ability to see things from a distance, and warned him that she might see them and warn her people. The king thought a little and then ordered his men to cut the big branches of the trees and carry them on their heads to deceive Zarqa al-Yamamah. He also ordered them to move at night only. This is what they did until they approached the Yamamah area.

When they approached, Zarqa al-Yamamah saw them and informed her people that the enemy was carrying trees on their backs. Her people did not believe her and started mocking her. When the enemies arrived, it was a big surprise to her people, and it was an easy win for the king's army. Later, they grabbed Zarqa Al-Yamamah and took her to the king, who asked her, "What did you see?" She told him, "I saw trees walking and behind them humans," so the king gouged out her eyes and ordered her to be crucified at the gate of the city. And that is how Zarqa Al-Yamamah became famous.

كان هناك ملك أراد أن يهجم على قبيلة زرقاء اليمامة لانه سمع عن نجاحهم و انتصاراتهم فأراد أن يثبت للجميع بأنه الأقوى . فقال له أحد أتباعه أن هذه القبيلة عندها امرأة اسمها زرقاء اليمامة وأخبره بقدرتها على رؤية الأشياء من مسافات بعيدة و أضاف : أخاف أن ترانا من بُعد وتحذّر قومها فيستعدوا لنا، فكر الملك قليلا ثم فكر في خطة و أمر الملك رجاله بأن يقطعوا أغصان الأشجار و يحملوها على رؤوسهم ليخدعوا زرقاء اليمامة، وأمر هم الملك بتنفيذ ذلك ليلا حتى لا تراهم زرقاء اليمامة و بالفعل قطع الجيش أغصان الأشجار و حملوها على رؤوسهم و كانوا يسيرون في الليل حتى اقتربوا من منطقة اليمامة .

عندما اقتربوا من مكان القبيلة شاهدتهم زرقاء اليمامه وقالت لقومها: لقد جاءكم أعداء يحملون أشجارا على ظهورهم فلم يصدقوها و صاروا يسخرون منها ، و لكن حين وصلت جيوش الأعداء كانت مفاجأة كبيرة لقومها و غلبتهم جيوش الملك، و حين دخل الجيش أمسكوا بزرقاء اليمامة و أخذوها الى الملك الذي سألها : ماذا رأيت؟ فقالت له : لقد رأيت الأشجار تمشي و خلفها بشر ، فقلع الملك عينيها؛ لتجنب خطرها وأمر بصلبها على باب المدينة ، وأصبح اسم زرقاء اليمامة من أشهر الشخصيات العربية

Vocabulary

Meaning	plural	word
Blue		زرقاء
Wide		فسيحة
Tribe	قبائل	قبيلة
See		رؤية
War	حروب	حرب
Enemy	أعداء	عدو
Get ready		يستعد
Reason	أسباب	سبب
Triumph	انتصارات	انتصار
Army	جيوش	جيش
Branch	أغصان	غصن
Tree	أشجار	شجرة
Believe		يصدق
Sight	أبصار	بصر

Meaning	plural	word
Happen		تحدث
Mountain	جبال	جبل
Cheer		يهتف
Greet her		يحيونها
Follower	أتباع	تابع
Implement		تنفيذ
Nighttime		ليلا
Actually		بالفعل
Make fun of		يسخر
Humans		بشر
Gouge		قلع
Crucify		صلب
Plan	خطط	خطة

المناقشة:

1. لماذا سميت زرقاء اليمامة بهذا الاسم؟

2. ماذا كانت تفعل زرقاء اليمامة لتساعد قومها؟

3. لماذا أمر الملك رجاله أن يقطعوا أغصان الاشجار و يحملوها؟

4. ماذا فعل الملك بزرقاء اليمامة ؟

قدّر ما تملك
Appreciate What You Have

Cultural Note

It is impossible to feel the value of grace if we do not appreciate what we have. We should not continuously look at the people around us who appear to have better lives and wish we were in their positions. If you obsess on other peoples' lives and believe that you alone struggle, you will only suffer stress and misery. However, if you were to exchange places with someone else, then you will discover that you are blessed in ways that so many people are not. We are all rich with what we have. We only need to appreciate it.

Practicing gratitude can lead to greater happiness and contentment. It's also important to understand that everyone has their challenges and difficulties, and it's rare for anyone to have a perfect life.

Translation

Once there was a student in elementary school. Every morning, his mother would prepare several sandwiches for him to take to school to eat at lunchtime. He was not happy with these sandwiches but after several months, he learned a very great lesson because of them.

The student used to sit next to his classmate who had many sandwiches and watch him enjoying his lunch. He found his own sandwiches to be tasteless, odorless, and cold. Therefore, he would not feel hungry and just left them in the bag as he sat and watched his classmates eat. It stayed like this for a good while.

After a few months, a new teacher came to supervise during lunch and she taught a lesson that he would never forget. This new teacher walked around, talking with the students and seemed to respect their opinions as if they were adults. She treated them as if they were her children and she was always smiling. One day, the teacher noticed that the student was upset and not eating so she came to him and asked, "Why don't you eat? Do you not have something to eat?"

كان هناك تلميذ في المدرسة الابتدائية ، كانت والدتة تعد له شطائر متعددة في الصباح ليأخذها معة الى المدرسة ليأكلها في ساعة الغداء . و لم يكن سعيدا بهذه الشطائر و لكن بعد عدة أشهر تعلم بسببها درسا عظيما جدا .

يقول هذا التلميذ: أثناء فرصة الغداء كنت أجلس بجانب زميلي الذي معه شطائر مختلفة و كنت أنظر اليه و هو يأكلها و الاحظ أنه كان مستمتعا بها جدا و كنت حين أمسك شطائري و أنظر اليها أجدها باردة بلا طعم ولا رائحة و لا أشعر بالجوع فكنت أتركها في الكيس وأجلس بدون أكل وبقيت على هذه الحال .

بعد عدة أشهر حضرت معلمة جديدة لتراقبنا و تجلس معنا في ساعة الغداء و عملت معي موقفا من المستحيل أن أنساه. كانت المعلمه الجديدة تتحدث معنا و تحترم رأينا كأننا بالغين . لقد كانت تعاملنا كأننا أبناؤها و كانت تبتسم دائمًا ، و في أحد الأيام لاحظت المعلمه أني أجلس منزعجا و بدون أكل فجاءت الىّ و سألتني : لماذا لا تأكل ؟ هل معك شطائر لتأكلها مثل زميلك؟

The student said, "Yes, but my sandwiches are not as tasty as his, and they are cold."

The teacher said, "Do you want to exchange your sandwiches with your classmate next to you?"

He said, "Yes," and was very happy with her suggestion.

She said, "OK, wait a minute."

The teacher went to his classmate, spoke with him for a few minutes, and then returned with his sandwiches. But when the student started eating them, he found them very ordinary, cold, and not as special as he had thought. A few minutes later, the teacher came back and asked, "How are the sandwiches? Are they as delicious as you expected?"

The student said, "No."

The teacher said, "I knew they weren't tastier than your sandwiches, but I wanted you to discover that yourself. I want you to understand that the problem isn't with your sandwiches, but with you."

"If you only focus on others, you will never enjoy what you have."

قلت: نعم و لكن شطائري ليست لذيذة مثل شطائره و هي باردة.

قالت : هل تريد أن تتبادل شطائرك مع زميلك الذي بجانبك ؟

قلت: أتمنى ذلك و كنت سعيدا جدا باقتراحها

قالت: حسنًا انتظر قليلا

ذهبت المعلمة الى زميلي و تحدثت معه بضع دقائق ثم أحضرت الشطائر التي كانت معه. و لكنني حين بدأت في الأكل وجدتها عادية جدا و باردة وليس لها طعم مختلف كما كنت أعتقد . و بعد عدة دقائق جاءت المعلمة و سألتني: كيف هي الشطائر؟ هل هي لذيذة كما توقعت؟

قلت: لا

قالت: كنت أعلم أنها ليست ألذ من شطائرك و لكني أردتك أنت أن تكتشف ذلك . أريدك أن تعلم أن الخطأ ليس في شطيرتك و انما الخطأ في داخلك أنت .

ما دمت تراقب غيرك فلن تستمع بما عندك أو بما تحضره أنت .

Vocabulary

Meaning	Plural	Word
Appreciate		قدّر
Own		تملك
Elementary		الابتدائية
Breakfast		فطور
Lunch		غداء
Dinner		عشاء
Beside me		بجواري
Pie, sandwich	شطائر	شطيرة
Enjoy		يستمتع
Taste		طعم
Impossible		يستحيل
Alone		بمفردك
Exchange		تبادل

Meaning	Plural	Word
I wish		أتمنى
Student	تلاميذ	تلميذ
Great	عظماء	عظيم
Colleague	زملاء	زميل
Chance	فرص	فرصة
Find		أجد
Situation		الحال
Her suggestion		اقتراحها
When		حين
I think		أعتقد
Expected		توقعت
Son	أبناء	ابن
Hunger		جوع

المناقشة:

1. ماذا كانت المشكله الكبيرة لهذا الولد ؟

2. كيف كان يأكل زميله في المدرسة ؟

3. كيف كانت المعلمه الجديدة؟

4. كيف كانت شطائ ر زميلة ؟

5. ماذا تعلمت من هذه القصة ؟

الثعلب و الثعبان
The Fox and the Snake

Cultural Note

Helping others is highly valued in the Arab world because it is considered a cornerstone of the Islamic faith, the region's predominant religion. Islam encourages everyone to help and support each other. In the Quran, there are many verses encouraging people to help one another and promises that those who help others will receive infinite rewards either in this life or the Hereafter.

Arabs and Muslims believe that giving to others will make you feel good because you just might change someone's life for the better. Helping others is a privilege that not everyone can do. It also makes you grateful that you have things that the needy do not have. It is also believed that the more you give, the more you will receive. Being kind to others may be a life-changing experience. But being kind and helpful does not mean you have to give something of monetary value. It may also be done by showing a positive attitude, through conversation, or even just smiling at someone.

Arabs also believe that being kind includes greeting people, visiting the sick, giving to charity, asking what people need and finding ways of assisting them, keeping the environment clean, feeding animals, and many other selfless actions.

Translation

There was once a man traveling in the desert on a cold winter day. As he traveled, he noticed that there was a snake on the ground shivering from the severe cold. Although the snake was venomous, the man felt bad for it so he picked it up and put it under his shirt to warm it. The snake snuggled up to the man's stomach and was very comfortable. Gradually, life returned to it.

After some time, the temperature rose, and the weather became warm.

The man lifted his shirt and said to the snake, "The weather is warm so you can return home!"

The snake looked at him and said, "No. I want to stay under your shirt. It's warm here, and I'm never leaving."

The man begged the snake to leave him alone, but the snake screamed at him, "If you try to make me leave, I will bite you and you will die immediately."

في يوم من أيام الشتاء الباردة كان هناك رجل مسافر في الصحراء و في طريقة رأى ثعبان على الأرض يرتجف من شدة البرد و مع أن الثعبان كان من النوع السام الا أن الرجل أشفق عليه و حملة و وضعة تحت فانيلته ليدفئة التصق الثعبان على معدة الرجل و أعجبه المكان المريح و عادت اليه الحياة

و بعد مرور بعض الوقت ارتفعت درجة الحرارة و أصبح الطقس دافئا . رفع الرجل قميصه و قال للثعبان ان الطقس أصبح دافئا و يمكنك أن تخرج من هنا و ترجع الى مكانك و تكمل طريقك !

نظر اليه الثعبان و قال: لا . أريد أن أبقى تحت فانيلتك فهنا المكان دافئ و لن أخرج أبدا

توسل الرجل إلى الثعبان ليخرج و يبعد عنه و لكن الثعبان صرخ في وجهه قائلا: اذا حاولت اخراجي من هنا فسوف أعضك و ستموت في الحال .

Because the snake was venomous, the man was not able to do anything but he began to think of a plan. He remembered that there was a fox known for its intelligence and ability to solve difficult problems. This fox was the judge of the area. So, he went to the fox's house, explained what happened, and told him that he saved the snake because he felt bad for it. He said, "It would have died if it had stayed out there in the cold, but now the snake is refusing to leave and threatening me that it will bite me if I try to remove it. Can you find a solution to this problem?"

The fox said, "Come to the court. We will sit together, I will listen to both sides and then I will decide. Both of you must stand before me."

When the snake heard the words of the fox, it came out from under the man's clothes and laid down in front of the fox on the ground.

The fox said to it, "I heard the man's story and I want to listen to your side. What is your point, snake?"

و لان الثعبان كان ساما سكت الرجل و لم يستطع أن يفعل شيئا و بدأ يفكر في حل . ثم تذكر الرجل أن هناك ثعلب معروف بذكائه و قدرته على حل الأمور الصعبة و هو قاض المنطقة . فذهب الى منزله و شرح له ما حدث و قال له : أنا أنقذت الثعبان لأنه كان سيموت لو ظل في مكانه و الآن هو يرفض أن يتركني و يهددني بأنه سيعضني لو حاولت اخراجه . هل بامكانك أن تجد حلا لهذه المشكلة ؟

قال الثعلب: تعالوا الى المحكمة و سنجلس معا و يجب أن استمع الى الطرفين ثم سأقرر و كلاكما يجب أن يقف أمامي حين سمع الثعبان كلام الثعلب خرج من تحت ملابس الرجل واستلقى أمام الثعلب على ألأرض

قال له الثعلب: لقد سمعت قصة الرجل و أريد أن استمع الى قصتك . ما هي وجهة نظرك أيها الثعبان؟

The snake said, "I am very comfortable inside his clothes, and the weather is very cold now, so why am I being asked to leave this warmth?"

The fox looked at the man and said to him, "I have heard the point of view of the snake. What do you want to do now?"

The fox then looked the as ax next to him and glanced at the man who understood what the fox meant. The man ran and picked up the ax and hit the snake on the head. This was the fox's judgment.

The moral of the story is that you should think of the consequences before you offer someone help.

قال الثعبان: لقد ارتحت جدًا في البقاء داخل الملابس الدافئة. والطقس بارد جدا في هذا الوقت فلماذا يُطلب مني أن أترك هذا المنزل الدافئ؟

نظر الثعلب إلى الرجل و قال له: لقد سمعت وجهة نظر الثعبان فماذا تريد لن تفعل ؟

ثم نظر الى الفأس الذي بجانبه و أشار بعينيه الى الرجل ففهم الرجل ما يقصده فأسرع و حمل الفأس و ضرب الثعبان على رأسه فمات على الفور وبذلك انتهت هذه القصة

الهدف من القصة أن تفكر قبل أن تساعد أحداً و تساعد من يستحق المساعدة فقط . .

Vocabulary

Meaning	Plural	Word
Snake	أفاعي – ثعابين	ثعبانٌ - أفعى
Shiver		يرتجف
Jungle		ادغال
Venomous		سام
Although		مع أن
Felt bad		أشفق
To warm		ليدفئة
Warm		دافئ
Continue		تستمر
Beg		توسل
Leave		تغادر
Stomach		معدة
Both of you		كلاكما
Axe	فؤوس	فأس

Meaning	Plural	Word
Travelling	مسافرون	مسافر
His undershirt		فانيلته
T-shirt	قمصان	قميص
Bite you		أعضك
Immediately		في الحال
Fox	ثعالب	ثعلب
Season		شتاء
Desert		صحراء
Cold		بارد
Although		مع أن
Bite		يعض
Immediately		على الفور
Weather		طقس

المناقشة :

1. لماذا حمل الرجل الثعبان و وضعه تحت ملابسة؟

2. كيف كان الطقس؟

3. لماذا لا يريد الثعبان أن يخرج من تحت ملابس الرجل؟

4. ماذا كانت ستفعل، الأفعى لو أخرجها الرجل، من تحت ملابسة؟

5. لماذا ذهب الرجل الى الثعلب ؟

6. لو كنت أنت مكان هذا الرجل هل ستساعد الثعبان ؟

الحياة لا تخلو من المشاكل
Everyone Has Their Own Problems

Cultural Note

With the spread of the media and technology, almost all people now compare their lives to others. We hear a lot of expressions such as: "Your life is so easy; you do not have to do this" or "You don't know what I'm going through." It's easy to compare our lives with what we see in others and wonder why our lives are not as comfortable as theirs.

However, everyone has their own problems, and everyone suffers in their own way. Almost all people wish to be rich, but having money is not the solution to our problems. Some might be dealing with not being able to put food on the table, not having transportation, losing a close family member, having a disease, or even needing to get good grades to earn a scholarship. In Arabic culture, no one would complain about their troubles in public.

We need to stop comparing our lives to others and be a positive influence on ourselves first. Comparing oneself to others can lead to negative feelings such as envy, dissatisfaction, and low self-esteem. It is important to understand that everyone has their own journey, challenges, and obstacles to overcome.

Translation

There once was a poor man who lived in a modest house. His next-door neighbor was a rich man who had the means to live a happy and luxurious life with many blessings. The poor man used to watch his neighbor without talking to him much and did not know anything about his private life. He felt bad that he did not have what his neighbor had.

One day, the rich man invited the poor man to dinner at his house for a special occasion with a group of his friends. The poor man was very excited and started counting the hours and minutes after receiving this invitation.

Finally, when it was time for dinner, he happily went to his neighbor's house. As he walked into the big backyard, he began to admire the large garden while looking at the various trees with many fruits, the flowers of different colors, and the various cars parked there. He began to think, "This really is paradise." Then, he entered the house and marveled at the large hall, the spacious rooms, and all the luxurious and beautiful furniture. He went to the dining room where the table held many kinds of meat, chicken, rice, and other delicious and varied foods.

كان يا مكان في قديم الزمان كان هناك رجل فقيريعيش في بيت صغير متواضع و كان يسكن بجانبه شخص غني و عندة كل وسائل الحياة السعيدة و الرفاهية و كثير من النعم ، و كان هذا الرجل الفقير ينظر الى جاره فقط و لا يتحدث معه كثيرا ولا يعرف أي شيئ عن حياته الخاصة أو مشكلاته ،و كان يتحسرفي قلبه لأنه لا يملك مثل ما يملكه جاره .

و في يوم من الأيام دعاه جارة الغني الى العشاء في بيته مع مجموعة من أصدقائه لان عنده مناسبة خاصة فرح الرجل الفقير و بدأ يحسب الساعات والدقائق في انتظار هذه الدعوة .

و حين جاء وقت العشاء ذهب الى منزل جاره الغني و هو سعيد جداً و حين دخل الى الساحة أعجب بها جدا و بدأ يتأمل بالحديقة الكبيرة و بالأشجار المتنوعة ذات الثمار الكثيرة و الأزهار المختلفة الألوان و السيارات المتنوعة و صار يفكر هذه هي الجنّة بعينها .
ثم دخل الى المنزل و بدأ يتأمل في الصالة الكبيرة و الغرف الواسعة و كل الأثاث الفخم و الجميل الموجود فيها . و ذهب الى غرفة الطعام و وجد الكثير من اللحوم و الدجاج و الأرز و أنواع أخرى لذيذة و متنوعة .

The rich man invited the guests to start dinner, and they began to choose what they wanted from the food. The owner of the house was looking at them and asking if they needed anything. Then, he called his servant and asked him to bring his own special food. The poor man was very surprised and said to himself, "Is it possible that there is food that is tastier than the food on the table and special to him only?" He kept watching the servant to see what special food the rich man would eat. After a while, the servant came with a small plate with a piece of dry bread and presented it to the owner of the house. The poor man couldn't believe what he was seeing and started rubbing his eyes to make sure that what he saw was real. Then, he asked the owner of the house about the reason for his different meal, and the man told him that he suffers from several diseases and cannot eat any of the delicious food. The doctor had told him that he can eat only dry bread. Then, the rich man went to another room to take medications for the diseases he suffers from. At that moment, the poor man realized that to have good health is a great blessing, and he thanked God very much that he has no pain or illness. He did not want to lose his health even for one day, because having good health is more valuable than all other things.

بدأ الضيوف يختارون ما يريدون من الطعام و صاحب البيت ينظر اليهم و يسألهم ان كانوا يحتاجون شيئا آخر ثم أمر خادمه أن يحضر له طعامه الخاص به . استغرب الرجل الفقير كثيرا و قال في نفسه : هل من الممكن أن يكون هناك طعاما ألذ من الطعام الذي على الطاولة و خاص له هو فقط ؟ و ظل يراقب الخادم ليعرف ما هو الطعام الخاص الذي يأكله الرجل الغني . و بعد قليل جاء الخادم يحمل طبقا صغيرا و فيه قطعة من الخبز اليابس و قدمة لصاحب البيت. لم يصدق الرجل الفقير ما يراه و بدأ يفرك عينيه ليتأكد أن ما يراه صحيحا . ثم سأل صاحب البيت عن السبب فأخبره أنه يعاني من المرض و أنه لا يستطيع أن يأكل هذا الطعام اللذيذ و أن الطبيب قال له ان بامكانه أن يأكل الخبز الناشف فقط . و بعد ذلك ذهب الى غرفة أخرى ليأخذ الدواء للأمراض التي يعاني منها .

في هذه اللحظة أدرك الرجل الفقير أن نعمة الصحة هي نعمة عظيمة و شكر الله كثيرا أنه ليس عنده ألم و مرض و أنه لا يريد أن يفقد عافيته حتى و لو ليوم واحد لأن ما يملكه هو أغلى بكثير من المرض .

Vocabulary

Meaning	Plural	Word
Rich	أثرياء	ثري
Beside		بجانبه
Means	وسائل	وسيلة
Humble	متواضع	ستواضع
Person	أشخاص	شخص
Luxury		رفاهية
Blessings	نِعَم	نِعمة
Special		خاصّة
Bemoan		يتحسر
Invite		دعى
Calculate		يحسب
Hour	ساعات	ساعة
Minute	دقائق	دقيقة

Meaning	Plural	Word
Garden	حدائق	حديقة
Productive		مثمرة
Luxurious		فخمة
Organized		مرتب
Guests	ضيوف	ضيف
Shock		ذهول
Plate	أطباق	طبق
Bread		خبز
Dry / hard		يابس
Rub		يفرك
Disease	أمراض	مرض
Waiting for		انتظار

المناقشة:

١. لماذا كان الرجل الفقير يتحسر على حياة جاره ؟

٢. ماذا رأى في بيت جاره و أعجبه كثيرا؟ (اكتب ٣ أشياء)

٣. ماذا كان طعام الرجل الغني؟ لماذا؟

٤. في رأيك ما هو الأفضل أن تكون غنيا و مريضا أو فقيرا و بصحة جيدة؟

استمتع بقهوتك
Enjoy Your Coffee

Cultural Note

In Arabic culture, coffee is an important symbol of hospitality and generosity. Coffee is native to Arab lands as it originated in Yemen and then moved to Saudi Arabia, Egypt, the Levant, and Turkey. Later it became popular in Europe and then worldwide.

When visiting an Arab family, it is tradition to be offered coffee. Usually, each person will be presented with two to three cups of coffee. The servings are not very big, a little like espressos. Some people like their coffee lightly brewed while others like it strong and dark. Some coffee is served with sugar if you like it sweet. However, traditionally, Arabic coffee is flavored with cardamom.

Translation

There was a university professor who, after he retired, regularly invited over a group of his former students who had graduated and started their working lives. He would sit with them, talk and listen to them, and ask about their work and achievements. In one of these meetings, the group of graduates at his house had achieved financial stability, succeeded in their working lives, and achieved prominent positions.

After greeting and talking about their school days and recalling beautiful memories, they started speaking about their work and complaining about the pressures at work that caused them stress.

كان هناك أستاذ جامعي و بعد أن تقاعد بدأ يدعو مجموعة من طلابه الذين تخرجوا من الجامعة و بدأوا حياتهم العملية. و كان يجلس معهم يتحدث و يستمع اليهم و يسألهم عن عملهم و انجازاتهم. و في أحدى هذه اللقاءات تقابل مجموعة من طلابه السابقين في منزله و كان هؤلاء الطلاب قد حققوا الاستقرار المادي و نجحوا في حياتهم العملية وكانوا يعملون في مراكز عالية

وبعد التحية و الحديث عن أيام الدراسة و استعادة الذكريات الجميلة بدأوا يتحدثون عن الضغوطات التي يواجهونها في أعمالهم و يشكون من حياتهم و عملهم الكثير لأنه يسبب لهم الكثير من التوتر و القلق.

The professor left to prepare coffee in the kitchen and returned carrying a large tray with a coffee pot and various cups, including large and small cups, luxurious cups, cups made of plastic and melamine, ordinary glass cups, and crystal ones. Some of the cups were very simple and cheap, while others were very beautiful and expensive.

The professor said to his students, "Please choose the cup you want and have some coffee." After each student chose their own cup, the professor said to them, "Look around you and see the cup each of you chose. Have you noticed that you chose only the beautiful and expensive ones? This is normal because we always want the best, and this is what causes you stress and anxiety. What you need now is coffee, not the cup, but you were looking for the most beautiful cup. I also noticed that you were watching what cups your colleagues were choosing. You wanted coffee and it didn't matter what the cup looked like. Look at life as coffee while jobs and money are the cups. In other words, social status is only cups; that is, they are just a means of life, and coffee is life itself."

"So, I advise you to enjoy the coffee and to not care about how expensive and fancy the cups look. The quality of life (coffee) remains the same and does not change, and when we focus only on the cup, we miss the opportunity to enjoy the coffee.

Consequently, I ask you not to pay attention to the cups and enjoy your coffee."

ذهب الاستاذ ليعد القهوة في المطبخ ثم عاد اليهم و هو يحمل صينية كبيرة عليها ابريق القهوة و فناجين متنوعة كثيرة منها فناجين كبيرة و صغيرة و فناجين فاخرة و أخرى مصنوعة من البلاستيك و الميلامين و فناجين زجاجية عادية و فناجين كريستال . بعض الفناجين كانت بسيطة جدا و البعض الآخر كانت جميلة و غالية جدا.

قال الأستاذ لطلابه تفضلوا اشربوا القهوة و كل واحد يختار الفنجان الذي يريده ، و بعد أن اختار كل طالب الفنجان الذي يريد قال لهم الأستاذ: انظروا حولكم و أخبروني ماذا اخترتم ؟ هل لاحظتم أنكم اخترتم الأكواب الجميلة و الغالية فقط؟ هذا شيئ طبيعي لأننا دائما نتطلع الى الأفضل و هذا ما يسبب لكم التوتر و القلق . ما تحتاجون اليه الآن هو القهوة و ليس الفنجان و لكنكم كنتم تنظرون و تبحثون عن الفنجان الأجمل و لاحظت بعد ذلك أنكم كنتم تنظرون و تراقبون الفناجين التي في أيدي زملائكم . أنتم كنتم تحتاجون الى القهوة و لا يهم شكل الفنجان .

انظروا الى الحياة كأنها القهوة و الى الوظيفة و المال كأنها الفناجين بكلمات أخرى : ان المراكز الاجتماعية هي الفناجين أي أنها مجرد وسيلة للحياة و القهوة هي الحياة وبالتالي فاني أنصحكم ان تستمتعوا بالقهوة و بعدم الإهتمام بالأكواب والفناجين

Vocabulary

Meaning	Plural	Word
Used to		اعتاد
Retire		تقاعد
Graduated	تخرجوا	تخرج
Practical		العملية
Graduate	خريجين	خريج
Leaving		مغادرة
Achieved		حقق
Position	مراكز	مركز
Kettle	أباريق	ابريق
Cup	فناجين	فنجان
Pour		يسكبْ
Worry		قلق

Meaning	Plural	Word
Achievements	انجازات	انجاز
Sentence	عبارات	عبارة
Greetings		تحية
Remembering		استعادة
Memory	ذكريات	ذكرى
Stress	ضغوطات	ضغط
Tray	صواني	صينية
Simple		بسيطة
Expensive		غالية
Choose		اختار
Petty		الشفقة
Stress		توتر

المناقشة:

1. من الذين دعاهم الأستاذ الى بيته؟

2. عن ماذا بدأ يتحدث الخريجون ؟

3. ماذا أحضر لهم الأستاذ؟

4. ماذا تمثل الفناجين ؟

5. ما رأيك في كلام الأستاذ ؟

6. ماذا تمثل القهوة؟

العقل ليس بالسن
Maturity Does Not Have an Age

Cultural Note

Most of the time, people look at children as immature and needing direction and support from adults. Maturity and intelligence are not solely determined by age, but rather a combination of experiences, environment, and personal growth. Encouraging and supporting individuals, regardless of their age, can help them develop their skills and reach their full potential. It is important to listen to their ideas and provide guidance where necessary, fostering a supportive and growth-oriented environment. You might meet an old man with no good ideas and a child with very mature and smart opinions.

It's true that maturity and wisdom can come from various sources. It's important to listen to and value the opinions of individuals of all ages. By doing so, we can foster a more inclusive and collaborative environment where everyone's ideas and contributions are valued.

Translation

Once, a young boy went to the bank every week and put £500 in his account. The employees were surprised so they told the manager, who told them that when he came again, to bring him to his office. The next week, the boy arrived to deposit £500 in his account. The employee told him that the manager wanted to see him, and they took him to the manager's office.

The manager asked him, "Every week, you deposit £500. Where do you get this money, as you are a young boy?"

The boy said, "I bet with people in the street and every time I win the bet."

The manager laughed and asked, "How do you do it?"

The boy said, "Would you bet with me £500 that I can kiss my eyes?"

The manager agreed, so the boy removed his contact lenses, kissed them, then reinserted them and took the manager's £500.

The manager was annoyed, but he didn't say anything. The next week, the boy came again to deposit his money. The manager stopped him and said, "You fooled me last week and took my money."

كان هناك ولد صغير يذهب الى البنك كل أسبوع و يضع 500 جنيه في حسابه، إستغرب الموظفون كيف يحصل على هذا المال و هو مبلغ كبير لولد في مثل عمره . أخبروا مدير البنك بالموضوع فقال لهم عندما يحضر الى البنك أخبروني و أدخلوه عندي في غرفتي، في الأسبوع التالي ذهب الولد ليضع 500 جنيه في حسابه الخاص . فأخبر الموظف مدير البنك و أخذ الولد الى غرفة المدير . قال له المدير : من أين لك 500 جنيه كل أسبوع ؟ من أين لك هذا المال و أنت طفل صغير ؟

قال الولد: كل يوم أراهن الناس في الشارع و أكسب الرهان.

ابتسم المدير وقال: كيف تفعل ذلك ؟

قال الولد: هل تراهنني على 500 جنيه انني أستطيع أن أُقبل عيني

قال المدير : نعم كيف ستفعل ذلك ؟

ضحك الولد و أخرج العدسات من عينيه و قبلها ثم وضعها في عينيه

إنزعج المدير من ذلك و أعطاه 500 جنيه و لم يقل له أي شيئ . في الأسبوع التالي جاء الولد مرة أخرى الى البنك و لكن المدير نادى عليه و قال له: لقد خدعتني وأخذت مالي و لم أقل لك شيئا

The boy said, "Let's make another bet. If you win, I will give you twice what I took from you last week." The manager agreed without a thought.

Then the boy said, "I need ten of your employees to witness our bet," and the manager agreed. When the ten employees came, the boy said to the manager, "I bet with you that your underwear is blue."

The manager laughed and said, "No, it's not blue."

The boy said, "It's blue."

The manager said, "No, it's not blue."

The boy said, "Blue," and the manager said, "By God, it's not blue." When the manager got tired of the boy, he got up, took off his pants and said, "I told you, it's not blue."

The boy paid the manager £1,000 and got up to leave. The manager stopped him and asked, "Why are you not angry that you lost? You just lost £1,000."

The boy replied with confidence and a smile, "Why should I be angry? I bet with these ten employees that I would make you take off your pants for £500, and I won!"

قال الولد: دعنا نعمل رهانا آخر اليوم . اذا أنت كسبت سأعطيك ضعف المبلغ الذي أخذته منك الأسبوع الماضي و اذا أنا كسبت فلن آخذ منك شيئا• وافق المدير و بدون تفكير.

قال الولد: أريد أن أحضر عشرة موظفين ليشهدوا على الرهان و وافق المدير •

بعد أن حضر الموظفين قال الولد للمدير: أراهنك على أن لون ملابسك الداخلية أزرق

ضحك المدير وقال :لا ليس أزرق

قال الولد: بلى هو أزرق

قال المدير :لا ليس أزرق

الولد يقول أزرق والمدير يقول والله ليس ازرق و أخيرا قام المدير ونزع بنطاله وقال: قلت لك ليس أزرق

سكت الولد ثم دفع للمدير 1000 جنيه، و قام يريد أن يغادر البنك و لكن المدير استوقفة و سأله : لماذا أنت لست غاضبا ؟ لقد خسرت 1000 جنيها ؟

ابتسم الولد و قال : لماذا أغضب؟ لقد راهنت هؤلاء الموظفين العشرة على أنني سأجعلك تنزع بنطالك مقابل 500 جنيه و قد فزت بالرهان !

Vocabulary

Meaning	Plural	Word
The bank	البنوك	البنك
His account		حسابه
Employee	موظفون	موظف
Manager	مدراء	مدير
I bet		أراهن
The bet		الرهان
I win		أكسب
I kiss		أُقبّل
Lenses	العدسات	عدسة

Meaning	Plural	Word
Got mad		إنزعج
Yesterday		البارحة
Underwear		ملابسك الداخلية
Pants	بنطلونات	بنطال
Confidence		ثقة
Yesterday		أمس
I won		كسبت
Witness	يشهدوا	يشهد

المناقشة:

1. لماذا استغرب موظفي البنك؟

2. من أين يأخذ الولد المال؟

3. كيف قبّل الولد عينه ؟

4. على ماذا راهن الولد في المرة الثانية؟

5. ما رأيك في هذا الولد؟

القاضي الذكي والشجرة المتكلمة
The Smart Judge and the Talking Tree

Cultural Note

Most cultures see greed as a reflection of selfishness as well as self-satisfaction. Arab culture is no different. As a result, Arabs encourage generosity and ask people to help and support each other. Several proverbs about greed are popular in Arab culture, such as "greed harms and never helps," "greed lessens what is gathered," "cleanse thy heart from greed and thy foot shall remain free from fetters," and "no gain satisfies a greedy mind."

Arabic folktales about greedy people often end badly for them because they lose sight of what is truly important in life and become consumed by their desires. This can lead to strained relationships, health problems, and an unhappy life. Greed can also lead to unethical behavior and cause harm to others, which is against the principles of many cultures, including Arab culture. It is important to keep a balanced and grateful perspective, to appreciate what one has, and to help and support others.

Once upon a time, there were two young men, Alaa and Zaher, who worked together. Alaa was honest and sincere with a very good heart while Zaher was deceitful, dishonest, and cunning. One day, the two young men went on a business trip. Alaa left to use the bathroom and found a bag of money, so he took it. When he returned, he told Zaher about the bag and said they would share the money when they returned.

However, Zaher wanted to take the whole bag for himself because he was greedy, so he thought of a plan. When they approached the city where they worked, Alaa said to Zaher, "Let's share. You take half of the money and give me the other half."

Zaher replied, "I have a better idea. How about we take only some of the money and bury the rest in a place that no one else will know about. And then, when we need money, we can take what we need." Alaa agreed to his proposal. So they took part of the money and buried the rest under a big tree.

كان يا مكان في قديم الزمان , كان هناك شابين اسمهما علاء و زاهر و كانا يعملان معا في للتجارة ، كان علاء أمين و مخلص و قلبه طيب جدا ولكن زاهر كان مخادع و كاذب و ماكر ، و في أحد الأيام كان الشابان في رحلة تجارية و في الطريق ذهب علاء ليقضي حاجته فوجد كيسا من المال فأخذه ، و حين رجع أخبر زاهر عن الكيس و قال له سوف نقتسم هذا الكيس حين نرجع.

ولكن زاهر أراد أن يأخذ الكيس كله لنفسه لانه طماع و مخادع و بدأ يفكر في خطة . وعندما اقتربا من المدينة حيث يعملان قال علاء لزاهر : هيا نقتسم المال خذ أنت نصف المال وأعطني النصف الآخر،

فأجابه زاهر: عندي فكرة أفضل . ما رأيك أن نأخذ بعض المال فقط و ندفن الباقي في مكان لا يعرفه أحد غيرنا ، و عندما نحتاج الى المال نذهب اليه و نأخذ ما نحتاجه منه ، و لأن علاء طيب صدّق زاهر و وافق على اقتراحه . و أخذا جزءً من المال و دفنا الباقي تحت شجرة كبيرة.

After several days, Zaher secretly went to the tree without telling Alaa and took the remaining money, then leveled the ground and wiped out all traces of his presence. After several months, Alaa needed money, so he told Zaher that he wanted to go to the tree. Zaher agreed and went with him. Alaa started digging and digging, but he couldn't find the bag or the money.

Alaa told Zaher, "You deceived me. No one knows about this money and where we buried it except us. You have taken the money."

Zaher replied, "You are the one who took the money." They kept arguing, and after a while, they decided to go to a judge to rule. Alaa told the story to the judge, and Zaher swore falsely that he did not take the money.

بعد عدة أيام ذهب زاهر إلى الشجرة سرا و دون أن يخبر علاء وأخذ المال المتبقي في الكيس ، ثم سوى الأرض و محا كل أثر له ، بعد مرور عدة أشهر احتاج علاء إلى المال ، فقال لزاهر أنه يحتاج الى بعض المال و يريد أن يذهب الى الشجرة و يحضر الكيس . وافق زاهر و ذهبا الى الشجرة و بدأ علاء يحفر و يحفر و لكنه لم يجد الكيس أو المال.

فقال علاء : لقد خدعتني ، و لا أحد يعرف بوجود هذا المال غيرنا لقد أخذت المال.

فأجابه زاهر: بل أنت من أخذ المال ،و بعد نقاش طويل قررا أن يذهبا إلى القاضي ليحكم بينهما ، حكى علاء القصة للقاضي و أقسم زاهر كاذبا أنه لم يأخذ المال .

The judge knew that Zaher was the liar, and he asked him, "Do you have proof that you did not take the money?"

Zaher said, "Yes. Ask the tree under which we buried the money and it will tell you that Alaa stole it."

The judge knew that trees do not talk but he agreed. The next day, they went to the tree. Zaher had asked his father, Abu Zaher, to hide behind the tree and fool the judge into thinking that the tree was speaking.

The judge asked the tree, "Who took the money? Was it Alaa?"

Zaher's father said, "Yes."

The judge wanted to teach Zaher a lesson that he would never forget. Therefore, he said in a loud voice, "Let's burn the tree so that it will tell us the truth." When Zaher's father heard this, he started screaming and shouted, "Please do not burn the tree!" and ran out from behind it.

The judge asked him what had happened, and Abu Zaher told him the truth. The judge ordered that all the money be returned to Alaa, and he flogged Zaher and his father as punishment.

و لأن القاضي يعرف أن زاهر كاذب سأله: هل عندك دليل على أنك لم تأخذ المال ؟

قال زاهر: نعم . اسأل الشجرة التي دفنّا تحتها المال و هي ستخبرك أن علاء هو من سرق المال.

وافق القاضي وفي اليوم التالي ذهبوا إلى الشجرة التي دفنوا المال تحتها و كان زاهر قد طلب من أبيه أن يختبئ عند الشجرة ، وأن يوهم القاضى أن الشجرة تتكلم.

فسأل القاضى الشجرة : من أخذ المال ؟ هل هو علاء ؟

قال أبو زاهر : نعم.

ولكن القاضي كان يعرف أن الشجر لا يتحدث و أراد أن يعلم زاهر درسا لا ينساه . فقال دعنا نحرق الشجرة حتى تخبرنا بالحقيقة و لكن عندما سمع أبو زاهر هذا الحديث ، أخذ يصرخ ويصيح و خرج من خلف الشجرة.

فسأله القاضي عما حدث فأخبره أبو زاهر بالحقيقة ، فأمر القاضي بإرجاع كل المال الى علاء وجلد زاهر ووالده عقابا لهم.

Vocabulary

Meaning	Plural	Word
Old times		قديم الزمان
Young guy	شباب	شاب
For trade		للتجارة
Kind	طيبون	طيب
Heart	قلوب	قلب
Cunning	ماكرون – محتالون	ماكر – محتال
Cheater	مخادعون	مخادع
Liar	كاذبون	كاذب
Found		وجد
We burry		ندفن
Honest	أمناء	أمين
Evidence	أدلة	دليل

Meaning	Plural	Word
Deceive		يوهم
Testify		تشهد
Wood		حطب
Use the bathroom		يقضي حاجته
Became closer		اقترب
Greedy	طماعون	طماع
Flogged		جلد
Idea	أفكار	فكرة
Secret	أسرار	سر
Trace	آثار	أثر
Delete/ erase		محا

المناقشة:

1. لماذا خرج علاء و زاهر ؟

2. ماذا وجد علاء ؟

3. لو كنت أنت من وجد كيس المال هل ستخبر صاحبك عنه؟

4. ما رأيك في موقف أبو زاهر ؟

5. كيف تصرف القاضي ؟

الأميرة والفقير
The Princess and the Poor Man

Cultural Note

It is common in the Arab world for people to hire household help to perform common chores including housecleaning, cooking, and watching after children. You do not have to be rich to have a maid. Middle-class families can afford one very easily. Servants and drivers are also hired from outside Arab countries, often from Asia. They usually live in the home in their own room. Depending on their contracts, they usually take leave to visit family annually or every three years. Various offices arrange for people to hire household help.

The problem is that servants are not always treated well. Some people might scream at them and punish them when they make mistakes. On the other hand, others can be very kind and supportive of their help and their families. For example, they might bring a husband and wife to serve as a driver and a maid or pay a dedicated servant more according to their needs.

Translation

Once upon a time, there was a wise and just king who ruled a very large kingdom. He had a very beautiful daughter who lived with him in the royal palace. The princess was arrogant and treated the servants harshly and despised them. She disrespected their feelings and constantly yelled at them. Her father, the king, was annoyed by her actions and felt very upset because he was a good king who loved everyone.

One day, the king heard her screaming at one of the servants and being very cruel to the man, so the king got very angry. He sat, talked to her, and asked her not to repeat the behavior. He said that if he heard her screaming at the servants again, he would not allow her to stay. Instead, he would marry her off to the first man to enter the palace because she must respect everyone and treat them politely. He hoped that by reprimanding her she would learn her lesson, come to her senses, and deal with people respectfully. At that moment, the princess regretted what she had done, but over time, she said to herself that her father would not let her leave the palace because he loved her, and he would not follow through on his threat. So, she returned to her old habit of being cruel and screaming at the servants.

A few days later, a young man came to ask the king for help in exchange for playing him music. The king agreed, invited him in, and asked him if he would agree to marry the king's daughter. When the princess found out, she begged her father not to have to marry this young man and said that she would change her bad behavior. She was crying and very sad. But the king refused and told her that he had given her more than one chance and yet she still did not change. He was determined to marry her off to this poor young man.

في قديم الزمان كان هناك ملك حكيم و عادل و يحكم مملكة كبيرة. وكان عندة بنت جميلة جدا ومدللة تعيش معه في القصر الكبير، و لكنها كانت مغرورة و تعامل الخدم بقسوة و تحتقرهم . و كانت لا تحترم مشاعرهم و تصرخ عليهم باستمرار. و كان والدها الملك يتضايق من تصرفاتها و ينزعج كثيرا لانه كان ملكًا طيبًا يحبُّ الجميع،

وفي يوم من الأيام سمعها الملك تصرخ على الخادم وتقسو عليه، فغضب منها و جلس يتحدث معها و طلب منها ان لا تعيد ذلك و أنه اذا سمعها تصرخ على الخدم مرة أخرى فانه لن يسمح لها أن تبقى في القصر و سيزوجها لأول رجل يدخل القصر لانها يجب أن تحترم جميع الناس و تعاملهم بأدب و احترام . في تلك اللحظة ندمت الأميرة على ما فعلت و لكن مع مرور الوقت قالت في نفسها أن والدها لن يدعها تترك القصر لانه يحبها و رجعت الى عادتها القديمة من الصراخ و القسوة على الخدم .

بعد عدة أيام جاء شاب يطلب المساعدة من الملك مقابل أن يعزف له على آلة موسيقية . وافق الملك و دعاة لمقابلته و سأله ان كان يقبل أن يزوجه ابنته .فرح الشاب كثيرا و وافق . و حين علمت الأميرة بذلك توسلت الى والدها أن لا يزوجها من هذا الشاب الفقير و أنها ستغير من تصرفاتها السيئة و كانت تبكى و حزينة جدا . و لكن الملك رفض و قال لها أنه أعطاها أكثر من فرصة و لكنها لم تتغير . وصمم أن يزوّجها لهذا الشاب الفقير.

The princess had no choice but to submit to her father, marry the poor young man, and then move in with him. His house was very small and far from the palace so she could not take anything with her except her clothes.

Living in her husband's house, she realized that she had to learn to wash dishes, clean the house, sweep the floor, and cook because she had no servant to help. She remembered her life in the palace and how she did not have to do any of those things. Her life completely transformed from that of a spoiled girl who did not do any work to the life of a person filled with misery and fatigue.

لم يكن أمام الأميرة الا أن ترضخ لوالدها و تتزوج من الشاب الفقير ثم انتقلت للعيش معه. كان بيته في مكان بعيد جدا عن القصر و كان بيتا صغيرا ولم يكن بامكانها أن تأخذ معها أي شيئ من القصر الا ثيابها

و حين عاشت في بيت زوجها أدركت أنها يجب أن تتعلم غسل الصحون و تنظيف البيت و مسح الأرض و اعداد الطعام لانه لم يكن عندها أي خادم ليساعدها و كانت تتذكر كيف كانت حياتها في القصر و كيف أنها لم تقم بأي من هذه الأعمال . لقد تحولت حياتها تماما من حياة البنت المدلله التي لا تقوم بأي عمل الى حياة الشقاء و التعب

Every morning, her poor husband would go to work early and ask her to cook food for him and have it ready when he returned, clean the house and the animal pen, and wash their clothes. At first, she was disgusted with all this work, but over time, she got used to it and became proficient in the tasks.

She added that if she could return to the palace, she would treat everyone there with kindness and respect. After hearing her words, the husband smiled and said, "I will tell you a secret that you would never imagine."

He said to her: "I am not a poor man; I am a prince like you, and my father is your father's close friend. Your father and my father agreed on this plan to teach you a practical life lesson, so you would learn to treat all people with kindness and respect because respecting others' feelings is extremely important."

The moral of the story is to highlight that arrogance is an unacceptable trait. No matter how high a person's status may be, they must remain humble and not look down on anyone.

كان زوجها الفقير في كل صباح يخرج للعمل و يطلب من زوجته الأميرة أن تعد له الطعام و يكون جاهزا في وقت عودته من العمل و أن تنظف المنزل و حظيرة الحيوانات و تغسل ملابسهم . كان يخرج في الصباح الباكر و يعود في المساء و كانت الأميرة تبقى لوحدها طوال الوقت . في البداية كانت تشمئز من كل هذه الأعمال و لكن و مع مرور الوقت اعتادت عليها و أصبحت تتقنها .

بعد مرور عدة أشهر على زواجهما عاد الرجل الى المنزل و وجد زوجته حزينة و بدأ يتحدث معها و يسألها عن سبب حزنها فقالت له أنها نادمة على معاملتها السيئة للخدم في قصر أبيها و على غرورها و على كل تصرفاتها الغير مقبولة. و أضافت لو كان بإمكانها أن تعود الى القصر فسوف تعامل كل من في القصر بأدب و احترام . بعد أن سمع الزوج كلامها ابتسم و قال سأخبرك عن سر لن يخطر لك على بال .

قال لها: أنا لست رجلا فقيرا و انما أنا أمير مثلك و أبي هو صديق والدك المقرب و أن والدك اتفق مع والدي أن يقوما بهذه الخطة لكي يعلمك درسا عمليا من الحياة و أن تتعلمي أن تعاملي جميع الناس بأدب و احترام لأن احترام مشاعر الناس هو أمر مهم جدا

الهدف من القصة هو توضيح أنَّ الغرور من الصفات الغير مقبولة أبدا و مهما كانت منزلة الإنسان عالية فانه من الواجب علية أن متواضعًا ولا يتكبر على أحد

Vocabulary

Meaning	Plural	Word
Spoiled	مدللين	مدلل
Arrogant	مغرورين	مغرور
Look down		تحتقر
Be harsh		تقسو
Bothered		ينزعج
Behavior	تصرفات	تصرف
Servant	خدم	خادم
Repetition		تكرار
Teach		يلقن
Respect		احترام
She regretted		ندمت
Threaten		يهدد
Musical instrument	الات موسيقية	آلة موسيقية
She begged		توسَّلت
Submit		خضع

Meaning	Plural	Word
Humble	متواضعون	متواضع
Cooking		طبخ
Washing		غسل
Cleaning		تنظيف
Dish or plate	صحون	صحن
She regrets		نادمة
Human being		إنسان
Misery		شقاء
Habit	عادات	عادة
Realized		أدركت
Barn	حظائر	حظيرة
Animal	حيوانات	حيوان
Plan	خطط	خطة
Insisted		صمم
Come to mind		يخطر على بال

المناقشة:

1. كيف كانت الأميرة تعامل الخدم؟

2. هل كان والدها يحب تصرفاتها؟

3. ماذا فعل الملك ليعلمها كيف نغير تصرفها؟

4. هل كان زوجها فقير؟

5. ما رأيك في خطة الملك؟

ليلى والذئب
Layla and the Wolf

Cultural Note

As mentioned earlier, the Arab family is considered the backbone of society. Family members have strong bonds and are always there for each other in times of need. They commonly visit and support each other. Extended Arab families can include as many as three or four generations. They provide material and emotional support, especially in emergencies. Grandparents are highly valued and extremely respected; they are seen as the sources of wisdom, and family members will seek their advice and guidance in important matters.

Note: There is another name for the story, "The Girl with the Red Robe," because she loved to wear a red robe or dress.

Translation

There was a girl named Layla who always wore a red robe, so everyone called her the girl in the red robe. One day, her mother told her to take a basket filled with some food, cakes, and medicinal herbs to her grandmother, who was sick. Layla put on her red robe, carried the basket, wore a hat on her head, and set out. Before she left, her mother told her not to go through the forest and to take the other path, as it was safer, because she was worried about her. However, Layla did not listen to her mother's advice and walked through the forest, singing and gathering colorful flowers for her sick grandmother. But then she heard a strange sound from behind the trees. She stopped to figure out what it was, only to be surprised by a large wolf jumping in front of her. Layla was very scared and started to tremble, causing the basket to fall from her hands onto the ground. The wolf ate some of the cakes and food, and then handed the basket back to her. Layla took the basket and thanked him.

The wolf asked her, "Where are you going?"

She replied, "I want to visit my grandmother, and she lives at the far end of the forest."

At that moment, Layla and the wolf heard a shot from a hunter's gun close by. The wolf fled immediately, and Layla began looking around, trying to figure out which way to go, only to realize she was lost. She sat down and started crying. The hunter heard her sobs and came to her, recognizing that she was the girl with the red robe. He went to her and asked, "Why are you crying? Why are you in the forest all alone? The forest is very dangerous."

كانت هناك فتاة اسمها ليلى و كانت دائما تلبس رداء أحمر اللون ،
لذلك كان الجميع يسمونها الفتاة ذات الرداء الأحمر، و في يوم من
الأيام قالت لها والدتها أن تأخذ سلة بها بعض الطعام و كعك وأعشاب
طبية لجدتها التي كانت مريضة . ارتدت ليلى رداءها الأحمر و
حملت السلّة و لبست قبعة على رأسها و خرجت، و قبل أن تخرج
قالت لها والدتها لا تذهبي من طريق الغابة و خذي الطريق الآخر
لأنه أكثر أمانا لأنها تخاف عليها . لكن ليلى لم تستمع لكلام أمها و
سارت في طريق الغابة و كانت تغني وتجمع الزهور الملونة لجدتها
المريضة . و لكنها سمعت صوت غريب من خلف الأشجار فتوقفت
لتتعرف على الصوت و لكنها فوجئت بذئب كبير يقفز أمامها . خافت
ليلى كثيرا و بدأت ترتعد فسقطت السلة من يدها على الأرض . هجم
الذئب عليها و أكل بعض الكعك و الطعام ثم أعطاها السلة .

أبتسمت ليلى و أخذت السلة منه فسألها : الى أين أنت ذاهبة ؟

قالت له : أريد أن أذهب لزيارة جدتي و هي تسكن في آخر الغابة

و في هذه اللحظة سمعت ليلى و الذئب صوت بندقية صياد و كان
الصوت قريبا منهما جدا فهرب الذئب و بدأت ليلى تنظر الى اليمين
و اليسار لتعرف أي طريق تأخذ فعرفت أنها ضلت الطريق و
جلست تبكي . سمع الصياد صوتها فجاء اليها و عرف أنها ذات
الرداء الأحمر فذهب اليها سألها : لماذا تبكين ؟ لماذا أنت في الغابة
لوحدك ؟ ان الغابة خطيرة جدا

He then added, "There is a dangerous wolf here, and I am trying to hunt it down."

Layla felt regret for not listening to her mother and for not taking the safer path. She said to the hunter, "I'm on my way to visit my grandmother, she is sick." So, the hunter took her to her grandmother's house.

While Layla was talking to the hunter, the wolf hurried to the grandmother's house and knocked on the door.

The grandmother asked, "Who is at the door?"

The wolf changed his voice and said, "It's me, Layla. I've brought you some food, cakes, and some medicinal herbs."

The grandmother opened the door and allowed him to enter. After a while, Layla arrived at her grandmother's house and knocked on the door. She heard a voice saying, "Come in."

But the voice Layla heard was not her grandmother's voice, so she hesitated. However, she thought to herself that perhaps her grandmother's voice had changed because she was ill, and she entered the house. The wolf had attacked the grandmother, put her under the bed, put on her clothes and glasses, closed the curtains to darken the room so it was harder to see and lay down on her bed.

After Layla entered, the wolf asked her to come closer. As she approached, Layla noticed that her grandmother's appearance had changed significantly, so she began asking her some questions.

ثم أضاف: يوجد ذئب خطير هنا و أنا أحاول أن أصيده

شعرت ليلى بالندم لأنها لم تستمع لكلام والدتها و لم تتخذ الطريق الآخر و قالت للصياد: أنا ذاهبة لزيارة جدتي فهي مريضة ، فأخذها الصياد الي بيت جدتها .

أثناء حديث ليلى مع الصياد ذهب الذئب مسرعا الى بيت الجدة و طرق على الباب.

سألت الجدة: من بالباب ؟

غيّر الذئب صوته و قال: أنا ليلى و قد أحضرت لك الطعام و الكعك و بعض الأعشاب الطبية

فتحت الجدة الباب وسمحت له بالدخول ، وبعد قليل وصلت ليلى إلى منزل جدتها و طرقت على الباب . سمعت ليلى صوت يقول لها: ادخلي.

لكن الصوت الذي سمعته ليلى ليس صوت جدتها فترددت و لكنها قالت في نفسها ربما تغير صوت جدتي لأنها مريضة و دخلت الى منزل جدتها . وكان الذئب قد هجم على جدتها و وضعها تحت السرير و لبس ثيابها و نظارتها وأغلق الستائر حتى تكون الغرفة مظلمة وتصعب الرؤية و تمدد على سريرها ،

بعد أن دخلت ليلى طلب الذئب منها أن تقترب منه ، فتقدمت ليلى ، لكنها لاحظت أن شكل جدتها قد تغير كثيرا فبدأت تسألها بعض الأسئلة.

Layla asked, "Why are your hands so long?"

The wolf replied, "So I can hug you and hold you close."

Layla continued, "Why are your ears so big?"

The wolf said, "So I can hear you better."

Layla then asked, "Why are your eyes so big?"

The wolf answered, "So I can see you clearly."

Finally, she asked, "Why are your teeth so big?"

The wolf said, "So I can eat you with them."

Suddenly, the wolf lunged at Layla, and she screamed and tried to escape. The hunter heard her cries, rushed back to the grandmother's house, and shot the wolf. He then searched for the grandmother and found her under the bed, rescuing her. Layla and her grandmother thanked the hunter very much for his help. The hunter then advised Layla to always listen to her mother's advice.

قالت ليلى: لماذا يداك طويلتان ؟

قال الذئب: حتى أعانقك و أضمك الى صدري

ليلى: لماذا أذناك كبيرتان ؟

الذئب : لكي اسمعك جيدا

ليلى: لماذا عيونك أصبحت كبيرة جدا ؟

الذئب: حتى أراك جيدا

ليلى: لماذا أسنانك كبيرة؟

الذئب : حتى آكلك بهم

و فجأة هجم الذئب على ليلى فبدأت تحاول أن تهرب منه و هي تصرخ فسمعها الصياد و عاد مسرعا الى بيت الجدة و أمسك بالذئب و أطلق عليه الرصاص ثم بحث عن الجدة و وجدها تحت السرير فأخرجها . شكرته ليلى و جدتها كثيرا على مساعدته ثم أوصى الصياد ليلى أن تستمع الى كلام والدتها دائما .

Vocabulary

Meaning	Plural	Word
Robe		رداء
Basket	سلال	سلة
Herbal	أعشاب	عشبة
Medical		طبية
Cake	كعك	كعكة
Hat	قبعات	قبعة
Safe		أمان
Flowers	زهور	زهرة
Colorful		ملونة
Wolf	ذئاب	ذئب
Shivered		ترتعد
Gun	بنادق	بندقية
Hunter	صيادين	صياد

Meaning	Plural	Word
Mother	أمهات	أم
Mother	والدات	والدة
Strange	غرباء	غريب
Right		يمين
Left		يسار
Dangerous		خطيرة
Added		أضاف
Regrated		ندم
Knocked		طرق
Drape	ستائر	ستارة
Bed	أسرة	سرير
Advised		أوصى

المناقشة:

1. ماذا كانت تحمل ليلى في يدها؟
2. لماذا ذهبت ليلى في طريق الغابة؟
3. كيف وصلت ليلى الى بيت جدتها؟ من ساعدها ؟
4. بماذا نصحها الصياد؟

الوالد و الابن
Father and Son

Cultural Note

Arab parents work hard to provide a good and happy life for their children and families. However, like many parents, they are sometimes so busy with their work that they forget how important it is to spend quality time with their children.

Parents need to strike a balance between providing for their children financially and emotionally. Quality time with children can help strengthen the bond between parent and child. Parents need to remember that material things can be lost or forgotten, but memories and experiences are priceless.

Additionally, quality time spent with parents helps children feel valued and loved and helps foster a strong bond between them. This can also be an opportunity for parents to teach life lessons and values that can instill good habits in their children. Of course, not all families have the same resources; however, it is important to focus on spending quality time with children. By prioritizing their children, parents can provide a supportive and nurturing environment that will help them thrive.

Translation

Once, a man returned home from work late at night, very tired after a long day. He found his five-year-old son waiting by the front door. The father looked at his son with curiosity and wanted to talk to him, so he began asking him questions.

The son said, "Can I ask you a question?"

The father replied, "Yes, of course. Ask me whatever you want."

The son asked, "How much do you earn per hour?"

The father, surprised, responded, "Why are you asking this? It's none of your business."

عاد رجل الى بيته من عمله في ساعة متأخرة و كان متعبا جدا بعد يوم طويل من العمل فوجد ابنه الذي كان عمره خمس سنوات ينتظره بجانب باب البيت . نظر الأب الى ابنه باستغراب و أراد ابنه أن يتحدث معه فبدأ يسألة .

الابن : هل تسمح لي أن أسألك سؤال ؟

الأب : نعم بالطبع . اسألني ما تريد ؟

الابن: كم تقبض من المال في الساعة الواحدة ؟

الاب مستغربا : لماذا تسأل هذا السؤال ؟ هذا ليس من شأنك .

The son said, "I just want to know, how much do you earn per hour?

The father replied, "If you really want to know, I earn 20 dinars per hour."

The boy was silent for a moment, looking down, and then said, "Father, may I have 10 dinars?"

The father, feeling very angry, said, "If you're asking me this because you want some money to buy a toy or something else, now is not the time. Go to your room and think about what you've done. This is selfish! You only thought about yourself and didn't consider me. Every day I spend long, exhausting hours at work."

The boy said nothing and quietly went to his room, closing the door behind him.

The man sat down in a chair to rest and his anger increased because of his son's question. He wondered why his son asked for money in this way if he needed it. Why didn't he just ask for money directly?

After some time, the man calmed down and began to think that perhaps he had been too harsh on his son. Since his son usually didn't ask for money, and he was his only child, maybe he really needed something. So he went to his son's room, opened the door, and asked, "Are you asleep, my son?"

الابن : اريد ان اعرف ارجوك اخبرني كم تقبض في الساعة الواحدة؟

الاب : أذا كنت مصمما ان تعرف انا أقبض 20 دينار في الساعة

سكت الولد قليلا و نظر للأسفل ثم قال : ابي هل من الممكن ان تعطيني 10 دنانير ؟

غضب الأب كثيرا ثم قال: اذا كنت تسألني لأنك تريد بعض المال لتشتري لعبة أو أي شيئ آخر فهذا ليس الوقت المناسب . اذهب الى غرفتك الآن و فكر فيما فعلته . هذا تصرف أناني ! أنت فكرت في نفسك فقط و لم تفكر بي . كل يوم أنا أمضي ساعات طويلة و متعبة جدا في عملي

لم يقل الولد شيئا و ذهب بكل هدوء الى غرفته واغلق الباب خلفه .

جلس الرجل قليلا على الكرسي ليرتاح قليلا و زاد غضبه بسبب سؤال ابنه و أخذ يفكر لماذا يسأل هذا السؤال اذا كان يريد بعض المال؟ لماذا لم يطلب مني المال مباشرة ؟

بعد مرور بعض الوقت هدأ الرجل قليلا و بدأ يفكر أنه ربما كان قاسيا على ابنه لأنه عادة لا يطلب منه مال و هو ابنه الوحيد و ربما هو يحتاج شيئا فذهب الى غرفة ابنه و فتح الباب وقال: هل نمت يا حبيبي ؟

The son replied, "No, father."

The father said, "When you asked me for money, I might have been harsh with you. It's been a long, exhausting day, and I took out all my frustration on you. Here are the ten dinars you asked for."

The boy smiled widely and said, "Thank you, father," then reached under his pillow to pull out the money he had been hiding there. The father looked at his son in surprise, thinking, "If he already had money, why did he ask for more?" Before he could say anything, the boy counted the money in front of his father and said, "This is twenty dinars. Can I buy an hour of your time? Please come home early tomorrow because I want to spend an hour with you and have dinner together."

الابن: لا يا أبي

الاب : حين طلبت مني المال ربما كنت قاسيا عليك لقد كان يوما طويلا و متعبا و لقد فرغت كل تعبي عليك . تفضل هذه العشر دنانير التي طلبتها . ابتسم الولد ابتسامه كبيرة و قال: شكرا يا ابي

ثم وضع يده تحت المخدة و أمسك النقود التي كان يخفيها هناك . نظر الولد الى ابنه باستغراب و هو يفكر: اذا كان معه مال فلماذا يطلب المزيد . و قبل أن يقول شيئا أمسك الولد النقود و عدها أمام والدة و قال لأبيه: هذه عشرين دينار . هل من الممكن ان اشتري ساعة من وقتك ؟ ارجوك تعال إلى البيت مبكرا غدا فأنا أريد أن أقضي معك ساعة و أتناول العشاء معك

Vocabulary

Meaning	Plural	Word
Late	متأخرين	متأخر
Tired	متعبين	متعب
Waiting		ينتظر
Allow		تسمح
Earn		تقبض
Not your business		ليس من شأنك
Let me know		اعلمني
Insist	مصممون	مصمم
Lend me		تعيرني
Borrow		تقترض
Hard	قُساه	قاسي
Dinar, currency used to mean dollar	دنانير	دينار
Selfish	أنانيون	أناني
Closed		أغلق
Directly		مباشرة
Pillow	مخدات	مخدة
More		مزيد

المناقشة:

١. لماذا كان الولد ينتظر أبيه عند باب البيت؟

٢. لماذا غضب الأب ؟

٣. هل اعطى الأب ابنة ما يريد من النقود؟

٤. ماذا يريد الابن أن يشتري ؟

٥. ما رأيك في تصرف الابن؟

جزاء سنمار
Sinmar's Reward

Cultural Note

Proverbs are brief sayings that teach a basic lesson or give important pieces of advice. Short, direct, and expressive, they are passed down from generation to generation. Sometimes, proverbs may be told in slightly different ways, but their messages remain the same. Arab culture is full of many beautiful proverbs.

This story is the source of a popular proverb that teaches that sometimes good deeds are rewarded with ungratefulness, punishment, or abuse: "the reward of Sinmar."

The lesson of this story is that you should be grateful for acts of kindness and that you should respond to people who treat you well with the thankfulness they deserve.

Some records indicate that al-Nu'man ibn al-Mundhir, the king in this story, was killed, as was Sinmar. Khosrow, the king of the Persians, invited al-Nu'man ibn al-Mundhir to a feast. However, Khosrow deceived him by poisoning the food in the same way that al-Nu'man ibn al-Mundhir deceived Sinmar. Therefore, he earned his punishment.

Translation

This story took place in the region of Al-Hira along the Euphrates River in Iraq. It is an old story dating back more than 1,500 years.

Once upon a time, there was a king named Al-Nu'man ibn Al-Mundhir. He wanted to build a grand palace that would impress all the other kings at that time and show off his glory. Al-Nu'man asked about the best engineers and builders in his kingdom and learned that the most skilled of all the builders was an architectural engineer named Sinmar, who was from Iraq.

The king sent for Sinmar, and told him, "I have called you to build for me a palace the likes of which has never been seen in my kingdom. I will reward you greatly."

Sinmar replied, "I am honored that you have requested me to build his palace. I will build you, my lord, a palace that people have never seen before, but I will need a thousand skilled builders."

The king said, "Request whatever you need, and you will have it in no time. The important thing is to complete the palace as quickly as possible."

وقعت هذة القصة في منطقة الحيرة بجانب نهر الفرات في العراق و هي قصة قديمه يعود تاريخها الى أكثر من 1500 سنة .

في قديم الزمان كان هناك ملك اسمه النعمان بن المنذر و كان من ملوك الحيرة. أراد أن يبني قصرا عظيما، يباهي به جميع الملوك في ذلك الوقت، ويفاخرهم. سأل النعمان عن المهندسين والبنائين في مملكته، فعلم أن أن أمهر البنائين جميعا مهندس رومي اسمه سنمار و هو مهندس معماري من سكان العراق .

ارسل النعمان في طلب سنمار فحضر لمقابلته. وقال النعمان:أرسلت في طلبك لتبني لي قصرا لم ير الناس له مثيلا في مملكتي، وسوف أكافئك مكافأة عظيمة

قال سنمار:يشرّفني أن يطلب مني الملك بناء قصره، سوف أبني لك يا مولاي قصرا ما رأى الناس مثله من قبل، لكن أحتاج إلى ألف من البنّائين المهرة

قال النعمان:اطلب ما تشاء، وستجده بين يديك في لحظات، المهم أن تنتهي من بناء القصر في أقصر وقت ممكن

Sinmar spent days and nights designing the palace with his assistants. He chose an excellent location by a river and began the construction. He worked tirelessly for several years, using his skills and experience to build the palace in a wonderful style. Once the construction was complete, Sinmar went to Al-Nu'man and said, "Your palace is now ready and awaits your arrival, my lord." King Al-Nu'man was delighted with the news and was eager to see the palace. When he saw it, he was greatly impressed and thanked Sinmar for his effort, skill, and artistry. He said, "I never imagined, Sinmar, that the palace would be this great and luxurious! You deserve a great reward."

A few days later, the king moved into his new palace and sent for Sinmar. Sinmar went to meet the king, who asked him to tour the palace with him and show him its rooms and halls.

Al-Nu'man and Sinmar explored every part of the palace and then climbed to the roof. The roof was high, and the view of the city from there was very beautiful. King Al-Nu'man asked Sinmar, "Is there a palace like this one?" Sinmar replied, "No, my lord." Then the king asked, "Is there any builder other than you who could build such a palace?" Sinmar answered, "No, my lord."

مكث سنمار ليالي واياما يعد رسوم القصر ومعه المساعدون، ثم اختار موقعا ممتازا على أحد الأنهار، وبدأ في البناء، واستمر يعمل ليلا نهار عدّة سنوات بلا راحة واعتمد فيه على خبرة عالية حتى أنه استطاع أن يبنيه بطريقة هندسية عالية الدقة . بعد أن انتهى من البناء، وذهب سنمار إلى النعمان وقال:قصرك جاهز الآن، ينتظر قدومك يا مولاي. فرح الملك النعمان بالخبر، وكان مشتاقا ومتلهّفا لرؤية القصر. و حين رأى القصر أعجب ببنائه كثيرا، وشكر سنمار على جهده وبراعته وفنّه، وقال ما كنت أتخيّل أبدا – يا سنمار – ان القصر سيكو بهذه العظمة والفخامة! إنّك تستحق جائزة كبيرة.

وبعد أيام انتقل الملك ليسكن في قصره الجديد، وأرسل في طلب سنمار. ذهب سنمار وقابل الملك النعمان. طلب النعمان من سنمار ان يتجوّل معه في جوانب القصر. وان يعرّفه بغرفه وقاعاته

طاف النعمان وسنمار في جميع جوانب القصر، ثم صعدا إلى سطحه. كان السطح عاليا، وكان منظر المدينة من سطح القصر جميلا جدا. سأل النعمان سنمار:هل هناك قصر مثل هذا؟. فأجابه سنمار:لا يا مولاي. ثم سأله النعمان:وهل هناك بنّاء غيرك يستطيع أن يبني مثل هذا القصر؟. أجاب سنمار: لا يا مولاي

Al-Nu'man thought for a moment and said to himself, "If this builder lives, he will build other palaces more beautiful than this one. There is only one solution. Yes, just one solution."

Al-Nu'man pointed to some of his soldiers and whispered an order to them. Immediately, the soldiers grabbed Sinmar and threw him from the roof of the palace! Sinmar fell from the great height to the ground and died instantly. This was the reward Sinmar received for his great work.

Since that time, the proverb, "the reward of Sinmar," is used for everyone who offers good to people only to be rewarded with evil.

فكّر النعمان سريعا، وقال في نفسه:إذا عاش هذا البنّاء فسيبني قصورا أخرى أجمل من هذا القصر. ليس هناك غير حلّ واحد. نعم. حلّ واحد

أشار النعمان إلى بعض جنوده، وهمس لهم بأمر. وعلى الفور، امسك الجنود بسنمار، وألقوه من فوق سطح القصر! سقط سنمار من الإرتفاع الكبير على سطح الأرض، ومات في الحال وكانت هذه المكافأة التي نالها سنمار على عمله العظيم

ومنذ ذلك الوقت، ونحن نقول هذا المثل:جزاء سنمار لكل من يقدّم خيرا للناس فيجزونه شرّا.

Vocabulary

Meaning	Plural	Word
Design		صمم
History		تاريخ
Engineer	مهندسين	مهندس
Architectural		معماري
Showing off		يباهي
Brag		يفاخر
Expert		أمهر
Reward		أكافئ
Palace	قصور	قصر
Helper	مساعدون	مساعد
Builder	بنّائين	بنّاء
Wander		يتجوّل
Throw him		ألقوه
Great		عظيم

Meaning	Plural	Word
Armenian		آرمي
Like it, same		مثيل
I am honored		يشرفني
Prepare		يعد
Accuracy		الدقة
Waiting		ينتظر
Imagine		أتخيّل
You Deserve		تستحق
Reward		جائزة
Went around		طاف
Side	جوانب	جانب
Roof		سطح
Go up		صعد
Wisper		همس

المناقشة:

1. لماذا أراد النعمان أن يبني قصرا ؟

2. هل أعجب الملك القصر ؟

3. هل هناك بنّاء غيرسنمار يستطيع أن يبني مثل هذا القصر؟

4. ماذا كانت جائزة سنمار ؟

5. لماذا أمر الملك بقتل سنمار ؟

القانون لا يحمي المغفلين
The Law Doesn't Protect the Fool

Cultural Note

There is a popular proverb that says, "Law doesn't protect the fool." It is a reminder to be cautious and wise, and not to place blind trust in others. Often, we find ourselves deceived, and the law cannot help us if we lack evidence and have simply trusted those around us. This proverb emphasizes the importance of being careful with our actions and words to avoid legal trouble or loss of property.

Experts agree that to be protected by the law, we need to be aware of our rights and regulations and act prudently. Here is a story from ancient Damascus in the Levant that illustrates the value of this proverb, though it does not explain its origins.

Translation

Once there was a poor woodcutter who every morning would go to gather wood, load it onto his horse, and then go to the market to sell it. This was his way of feeding himself and his family.

One day, after gathering wood, he went to the market to sell it. A group of merchants noticed him. One of them, known for his cunning and deceit, said to his companions, "Do you think I could buy this horse and all the wood it carries for just two dirhams?" His companions laughed and told him it was impossible, as the horse alone was worth more than forty dirhams. They made a bet on it, and the deceitful merchant went to the woodcutter.

He said to the woodcutter, "How much for this?"

The woodcutter replied, "Two dirhams."

The merchant asked, "Do you mean I can buy everything I see for two dirhams?"

في يوم من الأيام كان هناك حطاباً فقيراً و كان كل يوم في الصباح يذهب ليحتطب و يضع الحطب على حصانه ثم يذهب الى السوق ليبيع حطبه و كان هذا عمله ليطعم نفسه و أهل بيته

و في إحد الأيام بعد أن احتطب ذهب الى السوق ليبيع حطبه فشاهده مجموعة من تجار السوق. فقال أحدهم لأصحابة و قد كان مشهوراً بمكره و خبثة : هل تعتقدون أني أستطيع أن أشتري هذا الحصان و كل ما يحمله من الحطب بدرهمين ؟ ضحك رفاقه و قالوا له من المستحيل أن تقدر على ذلك . ان ثمن الحصان أكثر من أربعين درهم. تراهن التجار على ذلك و ذهب التاجر الخبيث الى الحطاب .

قال له: بكم هذا؟

فقال الحطاب : بدرهمين

قال التاجر : هل تقصد أني أستطيع أن أشتري ما أراه بدرهمين ؟

The woodcutter did not pay attention to the nature of the question and said, "Yes."

The woodcutter took the two dirhams, and the trader took the horse and the wood it carried. At that moment, the woodcutter shouted, "What are you doing? I sold you the wood, not the horse."

The merchant shouted back, "I asked if I could buy everything I see for two dirhams, meaning both the horse and the wood and you agreed."

The two men began to argue, and their voices grew louder. The crowd was divided between supporters and opponents until the police arrived and took them to the judge of Damascus at the time. The judge listened to the woodcutter and the merchant, as well as the witnesses. He realized that the merchant had deceived the woodcutter, but he ruled that the horse should be given to the merchant because the woodcutter had agreed to the sale and could not retract his agreement.

The woodcutter returned home very sad and told his family what had happened. His daughter said, "Father, don't be sad. Allah will reward us with something better than what we lost." A few days later, the woodcutter rented a horse to gather wood because he couldn't afford to buy another one. After collecting the wood, his daughter said, "I will go with you to the market to help you sell the wood." The woodcutter agreed, and he and his daughter went to the market. There, the woodcutter said to his daughter, "This is the place where the merchant took my horse, and this is the merchant who took it," pointing to him.

لم ينتبه الحطاب الى طبيعة السؤال و قال : نعم

أخذ الحطاب الدرهمين وأمسك التاجر بالحصان و الحطب الذي يحمله و حينها صرخ الحطاب : ماذا تفعل ؟ لقد بعتك الحطب و ليس الحصان

صرخ التاجر: لقد سألتك أن كل ما أراه بدرهمين يعني الحصان و الحطب

و بدأ الرجلان في المناقشة و ارتفعت أصواتهما و انقسم الناس بين مؤيد و معارض حتى جاءت الشرطة و أخذوهم الى قاضي دمشق في ذلك الوقت . استمع القاضي الى كلام الحطاب و التاجر ثم الى كلام الشهود و ادرك ان التاجر احتال على الحطاب و لكنه حكم باعطاء الحصان للتاجر لان الحطاب وافق على البيع و لا يجوز ان يتراجع

رجع الحطاب الى بيته و كان حزينا جدا و حكى لعائلته ما حدث معه فقالت له ابنته : يا أبي لا تحزن . سيعوضنا الله خيرا مما ذهب منا . و بعد عدة أيام استأجر الحطاب حصانا ليذهب و يحتطب لأنه لا يملك المال ليشتري حصانا آخر . و بعد أن جمع الحطب قالت له ابنته : سأذهب معك الى السوق لأساعدك في بيع الحطب . وافق الحطاب و ذهب هو و ابنته الى السوق و هناك قال الحطاب لابنته: هذا هو المكان الذي سلب فيه التاجر حصاني و هذا هو التاجر الذي أخذه و أشار الى التاجر

The daughter said, "Don't worry, Father. Go and rest for a bit; I will sell the wood."

The father left, and people started asking the girl about the price of the wood. She told them, "Ten dirhams," but they said the price was too high and left, commenting that no one would buy the wood at that price. The deceitful merchant overheard the conversation and approached her. He said loudly so everyone could hear, "I will buy what I see for 10 dirhams. Do you agree?"

The girl said, "Yes."

The merchant smiled, took out 10 dirhams from his pocket, and reached out to give them to her. The girl looked at him and said, "Is what I see the price of the wood?"

The merchant laughed and said, "Yes, all you see is the price of your wood."

So the girl then put her hand into her pocket and took out a knife. The merchant got mad and said to her, "What's wrong with you? Are you out of your mind?"

The girl said, "I want to be paid the price of the wood, which is your hand, and the 10 dirhams. I asked you, and you agreed!"

قالت البنت : لا تقلق يا أبي اذهب لترتاح قليلا و أنا سأبيع الحطب

ذهب الأب و جاء الناس و بدأوا يسألون الفتاه عن ثمن الحطب و قالت لهم: عشرة دراهم و كانوا يقولون لها أن هذا الثمن غال جدا و لا أحد سيدفع هذا الثمن و يتركونها و يذهبون و هم يتحدثون أن لا أحد سيشتري الحطب بهذا السعر . سمع التاجر المحتال كلام الناس فذهب اليها و قال بصوت عال حتى يسمعه جميع من حوله : سأشتري ما أري بعشرة دراهم فهل أنت موافقة ؟

قالت البنت : نعم

ابتسم التاجر وأخرج من جيبه عشرة دراهم و مد يده ليعطيها لها . نظرت البنت اليه و قالت: هل ما أراه هو ثمن بضاعتي ؟

ضحك التاجر و قال : نعم كل ما ترين هو ثمن بضاعتك

فوضعت البنت يدها في جيبها و أخرجت سكينا فخاف التاجر و قال لها : ما بك ؟ هل جننت ؟

قالت البنت : أريد ثمن الحطب يدك و العشرة دراهم . لقد سألتك و أنت وافقت !

Of course, the merchant refused, so the girl went to her father and told him what had happened. They, along with a group of good people who were in the market, went to the judge. When the judge heard the story, he was very pleased because he felt he had not given the woodcutter justice the first time. He then ordered his men to bring the deceitful merchant. When the merchant arrived, the judge said to him, "Everything you do will eventually backfire on you. Now, you agreed to give the girl everything she saw, which means your hand and the 10 dirhams. Since you agreed, you cannot retract the sale. You have two options: either we cut off your hand and give it to the girl, or you pay 1,000 dirhams as a ransom for your hand."

The merchant said, "I will pay the ransom. It is better than losing my hand." He paid the amount to the woodcutter and his daughter and left.

A thousand dirhams at that time was considered a large fortune.

و بالطبع رفض التاجر فذهبت البنت الى أبيها و قالت له ما حدث و ذهب معها مجموعة صالحة من الناس الذين كانوا في السوق و ذهبوا جميعا الى القاضي . حين سمع القاضي بالقصة فرح كثيرا لأنه شعر أنه لم يعط الحطاب حقة في المرة الأولى . فرح القاضي عندما سمع القصة لأنه لم ينصف الحطاب في المرة الأولى ثم طلب من رجاله أن يحضروا التاجر الماكر

حين رآه قال له : ان كل ما تفعله سينقلب عليك عاجلا أم آجلا . الآن أنت وافقت أن تعطي البنت يدك لأن جميع من جاء شهدوا أنك وافقت على اعطائها كل ما تراه و ذلك يعني يدك و العشرة دراهم و هي سألتك و أنت وافقت و لا يجوز أن تتراجع في البيع ! أمامك خياران : اما أن نقطع يدك و نعطيها للبنت أو تفتدي يدك و تدفع للبنت و أبيها ألف درهم . قال التاجر : سأدفع الفدية فهذا أرحم من أن أخسر يدي و دفع المبلغ الحطاب و ابنته و انصرف.

الف درهم في ذلك الوقت كانت تعني ثروة كبيرة

Vocabulary

Meaning	Plural	Word
Woodcutter		حطاب
Cut the wood		يحتطب
Group	مجموعات	مجموعة
More than		يزيد
Cruel	خبثاء	خبيث
Nature		طبيعة
Chaos		يتراجع
Police	شرطة	شرطي
The witnesses	الشهود	شاهد
Change his mind		تراجع
Will compensate us		سيعوضنا

Meaning	Plural	Word
Rented		إستأجر
The corner	أركان	ركن
Hide		توارى
Double	أضعاف	ضعف
Knife	سكاكين	سكين
Told		حكى
Happened		حدث
Pointed at		أشار
Stole		سلب
Price		ثمن
Choice	خيارات	خيار

المناقشة:

1. ماذا اشترى التاجر الخبيث بدرهمين ؟

2. ماذا حكم القاضي في المرة الأولى ؟

3. لماذا استأجر الحطاب حصانا؟

4. لماذا أخرجت الفتاة سكينا من جيبها؟

5. كم دفع التاجر لينقذ نفسة ؟

6. ما رأيك بتفكير الفتاة؟

جبينة
Jobaina

Cultural Note

This story is a tale from Palestine. The name of the girl in the story is derived from the word "cheese" in Arabic. It tells the story of a very beautiful fair-skinned Palestinian girl. The phrase "She is as white as cheese" was once a common expression used to describe someone with very fair skin. The story was crafted when most of the cheese that was produced was white.

The tale also reflects cultural practices. In the past, children needed their parents' permission before traveling, especially out of town, and could not go without their approval. Another aspect of the story highlights a traditional wedding custom still practiced today. On the wedding day, the groom's family and close friends gather at his house to sing and dance before parading to the bride's home.

The procession is filled with singing, music, and merriment. Upon arrival, the bride's father and a close male relative will join the groom, and a family member will drive them to the reception hall. Historically, the wedding celebration took place at the groom's family's house, where everyone would come together to celebrate.

Translation

Once upon a time, there was a woman who lived in a Palestinian village. She did not have any children. One day, a man selling cheese passed by her house, walking between the homes and calling out loudly: "White cheese for sale, white cheese for sale, come and buy white cheese."

When he passed by her house, the woman opened the door and bought some cheese from him. As she looked at the cheese, she prayed, "Oh Lord, grant me a beautiful daughter as white as this cheese."

After some time, the woman became pregnant and gave birth to a daughter as white as cheese so they called her Jobaina. When Jobaina grew up, she became one of the most beautiful girls in the village.

One day, there was a wedding in a neighboring village. It was customary for a group of the groom's family and friends to go to the bride's house to bring her to the wedding. They would sing and dance most of the way. Some of Jobaina's friends wanted to go to the bride's village and join the celebration, and they asked her to go with them.

She said, "You must ask my mother." So, they went to ask her mother, who replied, "Ask her father."

في قديم الزمان كان هناك امرأة تعيش في قرية فلسطينية . بعد مرور عدة أعوام على زواجها لم تحمل و لم يكن عندها أولاد . و في يوم من الأيام مرّ بجانب بيتها رجل يبيع الجبنة و كان يمشي بين البيوت و ينادي بصوت عال: جبنه بيضاء للبيع , جبنه للبيع تعالوا اشتروا جبنه بيضاء .

فتحت المرأة الباب و اشترت بعض الجبن منه و حين نظرت الى الجبنه دعت: يا رب أرزقني بنت جميله و بيضاء مثل هذه الجبنة .

بعد فترة حملت هذه السيدة و ولدت بنت بيضاء مثل الجبنه فاطلقت عليها اسم «جبينه» و حين كبرت جبينة أصبحت من أجمل بنات القرية .

و في يوم كان هناك عرس في القرية المجاورة و العادة هناك أن تذهب مجموعة من أهل و أصحاب العريس الى المكان الذي تعيش فيه العروس ليحضروها من بيت أبيها و كانوا يغنون و يرقصون طوال الطريق . فأرادت صاحبات جبينة أن يذهبن الى بلد العروس و يشاركن في الاحتفال و قالوا لها أن تذهب معهم .

قالت: يجب أن تسألوا أمي. فذهبوا لسؤال أمها فقالت لهم: اسألوا أبوها

So, they went to her father at his farm to ask him, and he said, "Yes, she can go with you, but please take care of her and do not leave her alone on the road." They went to Jobaina and told her to get ready to go with them since her father had agreed. Jobaina was very happy and started preparing. Jobaina's mother sent their maid along to look after her and gave her a bead, saying, "If you need anything, speak to the bead, and I will hear you. This bead is magical."

Jobaina was excited about the trip and the bead. After several hours, the maid said, "I'm tired from walking. Let me ride on the horse!"

Jobaina placed the bead near her mouth and said to it, "Mother, the maid wants me to get off so she can ride instead." Her mother replied, "Don't get off," and the mother shouted at the maid "Keep walking!"

Every now and then, the maid would ask Jobaina to get down so she could ride in her place. Jobaina continued to ask her mother, who rejected the idea every time. The mother was afraid that Jobaina would get tired.

After a while, they reached a river. Jobaina got off to drink and accidentally dropped the bead into the river. When the maid saw that the bead had fallen, she laughed and said to Jobaina, "Now you are the maid, and I am your lady." She smeared herself with white dirt to appear fair and coated Jobaina with black soot so no one would recognize her. Then, she mounted the horse, changed the route, and headed towards the sultan's palace.

فذهبوا الى أبوها في مزرعته ليسألوه فقال لهم: نعم ممكن أن تذهب معكم و لكن انتبهوا لها و لا تتركوها لوحدها في الطريق . فذهبوا الى جبينة و أخبروها أن تستعد للذهاب معهم لأن أبوها وافق . فرحت جبينه كثيرا و بدأت بالاستعداد . أم جبينه أرسلت معها خادمة لتهتم بها و أعطتها خرزة و قالت لها : اذا احتجت أي شيئ كلمي الخرزة و سوف أسمعك فهذه خرزة سحرية

كانت جبينه سعيدة بالرحلة و بالخرزة . و بعد مرور عدة ساعات قالت الخادمة لها: لقد تعبت من المشي دعيني أركب مكانك على الحصان .

وضعت جبينه الخرزة بالقرب من فمها و قالت للخرزة: يا أمي الخادمة تريدني أن أنزل و هي تركب مكاني قالت أمها : لا تنزلي و صرخت على الخادمة : استمري في المشي

و استمرت الخادمة تطلب من جبينه أن تنزل لتركب هي مكانها على الحصان و استمرت جبينه تسأل أمها التي كانت ترفض الفكرة في كل مرة. كانت الأم تخاف على جبينه و لا تريدها أن تتعب

بعد مرور بعض الوقت وصلوا الى نهر و نزلت جبينه لتشرب و وقعت الخرزة منها في النهر . و حين رأت الخادمة أن الخرزة وقعت ضحكت و قالت لجبينه : الآن أنت الخادمة و انا سيدتك . و دهنت نفسها ببعض التراب الأبيض لتبدو بيضاء و دهنت جبينه بسخام أسود حتى لا يعرفها أحد و ركبت على الحصان و غيرت الطريق و ذهبت للمنطقة التي يوجد بها قصر السلطان .

The sultan's son saw them and instructed one of his attendants to go and bring both girls to the palace. The attendant went and invited the girls to the palace. After some time, the sultan's son married the maid and assigned Jobaina to tend the sheep. Jobaina took care of the sheep, but they began to weaken day by day. The sultan's son was puzzled and decided to observe Jobaina to understand what was causing the problem. As he followed her, he heard her singing and crying with the following song:

"Birds flying, and wandering beasts,

Tell my mother and father, Jobaina has become a shepherdess.

She herds sheep and herds camels,

And naps under the grape vines."

The sultan's son went to Jobaina and asked her about her story and the reason for her tears. She told him everything. He then gathered the people in his area and declared that Jobaina was now the lady of the palace and that he would punish her maid severely. Jobaina lived in the palace, married the son of the sultan, and they lived happily ever after.

رآها ابن السلطان و قال لأحد أتباعه أن يذهب و يحضر البنتين فذهب و دعا البنتين الى القصر . بعد فترة من الزمن تزوج ابن السلطان من الخادمة طلب من جبينة أن ترعى الغنم . صارت جبينة ترعى الغنم و لكن الغنم بدأت تضعف يوما بعد يوم .

استغرب ابن السلطان و قرر أن يراقب جبينه ليرى ماذا تفعل ليعرف السبب . و حين تبعها سمعها تغني هذه الأغنية و تبكي :

يا طيور طايرة ويا وحوش سايرة

قولي لامي وابوي جبينة صارت راعية

ترعى غنم وترعى نوق

وتقيّل تحت الدالية

فذهب ابن السلطان الى جبينه و سألها عن قصتها و سبب بكاءها فأخبرته بقصتها كاملة فجمع ابن السلطان الناس في منطقته و قال لهم أن جبينه هي سيدة القصر الآن و أنه سوف يعاقب خادمتها عقابا شديدا . و عاشت جبينه في القصر وبعد فترة من الزمن تزوجت من ابن السلطان و أحضرت أهلها ليعيشوا معها في القصر .

Vocabulary

Meaning	Plural	Word
Village	قرى	قرية
Get pregnant		تحمل
Sell		يبيع
Calling		ينادي
Cheese		جبنة
Between		بين
Come		تعال
Lady	سيدات	سيدة
Buy		يشتري
Give me		ارزقني
Oh God		يا رب
Give birth		ولدت
Bride	عرايس	عروس
Groom	عريسان	عريس
Wedding	أعراس	عرس

Meaning	Plural	Word
Sing		يغني
Dance		يرقص
Culture		العادة
Bead	خرزات	خرزة
Magical		سحرية
Sultan	سلاطين	سلطان
Sand		تراب
Black soot		سخام أسود
River	أنهار	نهر
Shepard		ترعى
Sheep	أغنام	غنم
Camel	نوق	ناقة
Deltoid		دالية
Horse	أحصنة	حصان

المناقشة:

1. ماذا دعت الأم ؟

2. لماذا سمت ابنتها جبينه؟

3. أين ذهبت جبينه مع صديقاتها؟

4. ماذا حدث لخرزة جبينة؟

5. هل هناك خرزة سحرية؟

6. ماذا تشبه الخرزة في عصرنا الحاضر ؟

ستحصد ما تزرع
You Will Reap What You Sow

Cultural Note

In the past, running water was not available in streets, shops, or markets. As a result, some people took on the task of selling water in these areas, carrying large containers and offering drinks in cups. These water vendors were known for their friendly demeanor, always smiling and sharing stories to attract customers. They were skilled salespeople in their own right.

This is a story about a butler whose good manners and kind heart ultimately saved his life.

Translation

Once upon a time, there was a butler named Mohammad who was known for his good manners and conversation skill. He was well-loved and renowned among the people in the area, to the point that his fame reached the king. One day, the king told his minister that he had heard great things about the butler Mohammad and ordered him to bring Mohammad to the palace. The king wanted Mohammad to serve as the palace water bearer so that he could enjoy his stories and pleasant conversation.

The minister went to Mohammad and conveyed the king's message. Mohammad was overjoyed and immediately went home to share the exciting news with his wife and children. The family was happy. The next morning, he went to the palace, where he started his new job. Mohammad grew quite close to the king.

However, Mohammad's close relationship with the king made the minister very jealous. The minister began to devise a plot against Mohammad to keep him away from the king. One day, as Mohammad was leaving the palace, the minister waited for him at the door and said, "The king is bothered by the bad smell of your breath."

Mohammad asked, "What do you suggest I do to get rid of this odor?"

The minister replied, "Cover your mouth with a mask."

في قديم الزمان كان هناك رجل اسمه محمد يبيع الماء و يتمتع بالخلق الكريم و الكلام الحسن . كان محبوبا و مشهورا بين زبائنه و أصحابه حتى أن شهرته وصلت إلى الملك، وفي يوم من الأيام قال الملك لوزيره بأنه سمع كلاما جيدا عن الساقي محمد و أمرة بأن يحضره الى القصر لكي يعمل ساقيا داخل القصر حتى يستمتع الملك و من معه بالقصر بقصصه وحكاياته و كلامه الجميل

ذهب الوزير إلى الساقي محمد و أخبره بما قال له الملك ففرح محمد كثيرا و ذهب مباشرة الى زوجته و أولاده ليبشرهم بهذا الخبر السعيد و فرحت العائله كثيرا. و في صباح اليوم التالي ذهب محمد الى قصر الملك وبدأ يقدم الماء للملك و لجميع من في القصر ثم يذهب و يجلس مع الملك بالقصر و يحكي له بعض القصص . أُعجب الملك بحديث محمد و أصبح قريبا منه كثيراً

كانت علاقة محمد بالملك تجعل الوزير يغار كثيرا من محمد و أخذ يفكر في خدعة حتى يبعده عن الملك . و في يوم و حين كان محمد قد أنهى عمله اليومي و خارجا من القصر نادى عليه و قال له: ان الملك تؤذيه رائحة فمك الكريهه .

قال محمد: ما رأيك ؟ ماذا أفعل لأتخلص من هذه الرائحة ؟

قال الوزير: ضع لثام على فمك

When the king saw him, he was puzzled but said nothing. Mohammad continued this way for several days. Eventually, the king asked the minister about the reason for Mohammad's mask. The minister, pretending he was afraid, requested the king's promise not to harm or kill him if he revealed the truth. The king assured him that he would not harm him. The minister then said, "Mohammad complains about the bad smell of your breath, and he is wearing the mask to avoid smelling it."

The king was very angry upon hearing this from the minister. When he returned to his wife and told her what the minister had said, she was also furious and said that no one in the kingdom should dare insult her husband and she said that whoever dared to offend the king must die. The king agreed with his wife and decided to kill Mohammad.

The next morning, before Mohammad arrived, the king summoned the executioner and instructed him to wait at the palace gate and behead anyone who left the palace carrying a flowers. The executioner went to the door to wait.

Later, Mohammad arrived at the palace, completed his daily duties, and, as he was about to leave, the king gave him a bouquet of flowers. On his way out, the minister stopped him and asked about the bouquet. Mohammad told him that they were a gift from the king. The minister took the bouquet from him, saying he was more deserving of it, and left. At the door, the executioner saw the minister with the flowers, so he cut off his head.

وافق محمد على اقتراح الوزير و في صباح اليوم التالي وضع اللثام على فمه و ذهب الى القصر . حين رآه الملك استغرب كثيرا و لكنه لم يقل شيئا و استمر على هذه الحال لعدة أيام فقام الملك بسؤال الوزير عن سبب استخدام محمد للثام على وجهه فتظاهر الوزير بالخوف و طلب من الملك أن يعده بأنه لن يؤذيه أو يقتله حين يخبره عن السبب فوعده الملك أن لا يؤذيه بأي شكل من الأشكال . فقال الوزير : ان محمد يشتكي من رائحة فمك الكريهة و هو يضع اللثام حتى لا يشمها .

غضب الملك كثيرا مما سمعه من الوزير وعندما عاد إلى زوجته و حدثها بما سمعه من الوزير غضبت أيضا و قالت لا يجوز أن يتجرأ أي انسان في المملكه على الملك يجب أن يكون جزاء محمد الموت حتى يكون عبرة لغيرة . وافق الملك و أعجبته الفكرة .

في صباح اليوم التالي نادى الملك على السياف و قال له أن ينتظر عند باب القصر و أن يقطع رأس من يخرج من القصر و هو يحمل باقة من الزهور . و فعلا ذهب السياف ينتظر عند باب القصر.

و حضر محمد الى القصر و قام بعملة اليومي و عندما جاء موعد مغادرته و ذهابه الى البيت أعطاه الملك باقة من الزهور . فرح محمد و حمل الباقة و قبل أن يصل الى الباب رآه الوزير ساله عن باقة الزهور فقال له محمد أنها من الملك فأخذها منه و قال له أنا أحق بها منك . و حين خرج من الباب كان السياف في الانتظار و قطع رأسه

The next morning, Mohammad went to the palace. When the king saw him, he was very surprised and called him into his office. The king asked about the reason for the mask, and Mohammad explained that the minister had told him that the king was bothered by the bad smell of his breath and had advised him to wear the mask to avoid it. The king then inquired about the bouquet of flowers and what had happened to it. Muhammad told him that the minister had taken it from him, claiming he was more deserving of it.

The king smiled and said to himself, "Yes, he deserved it."

في صباح اليوم التالي ذهب محمد الى القصر و حين رآه الملك استغرب كثيرا فدعاه الى مكتبه و سأله عن قصة اللثام فاخبره بمحمد بما قاله الوزير من أن جلالته تؤذيه رائحة فمة و نصحه بأن يضع لثام على فمه لمنع الرائحة، اثم سأله الملك عن باقة الزهور و ماذا فعل بها فقال له محمد أن الوزير أخذها منه و قال له أنه هو أحق بها .

ابتسم الملك و قال له :: فعلا انه أحق بها لأنه ظلمك

Vocabulary

Meaning	Plural	Word
Butler	سقاة	ساقي
Enjoy		يتمتع
Popular		محبوب
Customer	زبائنه	زبون
Summoned		استدعى
Ordered him		أمره
Feel happy		فرح
Heralds, tells good news		يبشر
Close		قريب
Jealousy		غيرة
Plot		يكيد
Bothered		يتأذى

Meaning	Plural	Word
Hateful		كريهة
Get over		التغلب
Mask		لثام
Pretend		اظهر
Your majesty	جلالتكم	جلالتك
Dare		يتجرأ
Kill		قتل
Head cutter (using a sword)		السياف
He stopped him		استوقفه
Directly		مباشرة
Bouquet	باقات	باقة
Direct		مباشرة

المناقشة:

1. ماذا كان يعمل محمد؟

2. لماذا أراد الملك أن يعمل محمد ساقيا في القصر؟

3. لماذا أراد الوزير أن يتخلص من محمد؟

4. لماذا لبس محمد لثاما على وجهه؟

5. لماذا غضب الملك من محمد؟

6. ما رأيك في نهاية القصة؟

الفتى وشجرة التفاح
The Apple Tree and the Boy

Cultural Note

We have countless blessings that often go unrecognized because we simply live and experience them as part of life. Many people lack the very things we take for granted, yet we rarely pause to appreciate them. In Arab culture, parents are considered the greatest blessings that children have, as they provide for them throughout their lives.

This story illustrates the many blessings that parents offer their children. The boy in the story continuously takes and requests from his parents, accustomed to their constant support. Even as his parents grow old and can no longer meet his needs, he still turns to them for help, because deep down, he knows they are the source of his happiness and support.

Translation

Once upon a time, there was a huge apple tree with large branches, tall and extended limbs, and beautiful green leaves. The tree was full of sweet apples and had a strong trunk.

A boy came and began playing around the tree. He would spend all day climbing it, running around it, eating its fruit when he was hungry, and resting under its shade when he was tired. The boy spent all day, every day doing this.

Later, when the boy got a little older, he stopped going to the apple tree. Years passed while the tree was waiting patiently for him to come back. One day, the boy returned and sat under the tree, but he did not play like he used to.

كانت هناك شجرة تفاح ضخمة ذات فروع كبيرة وأغصان طويلة و عالية وأوراق خضراء جميلة، و كانت مليئة بثمار التفاح و مذاقها لذيذ جدا ، وكانت تلك الشجرة تمتلك جذعاً قوياً و كبيرا.

في يوم من الأيام جاء ولد و بدأ يلعب حول الشجرة و كان يقضي طوال اليوم يصعد فوقها و يجري حولها و يأكل من ثمرها حين يجوع و ينام تحت ظلها حين يشعر بالتعب . كان يفعل ذلك كل يوم لسنوات عديدة .

ثم توقف الولد عن الذهاب الى الشجرة التي كانت تنتظره بفارغ الصبر . و في يوم من الأيام عاد الولد الى الشجرة و لكنه لم يلعب كعادته و انما جلس تحت ظلها

The tree asked him, "Why are you not playing with me?"

The boy replied, "I have a problem. I want to buy many things, but I don't have the money to pay for them."

The tree said, "You can pick up some apples from my branches, sell them, and buy what you need with the money you get."

The boy was very happy with the idea. He collected the apples and went to sell them. He was very excited. However, he did not go back to the tree, and the tree was sad.

Many months went by before the boy returned to the tree. When he came back, he sat under it and did not play. When the tree asked him why, he said, "I am now a grown man with a family to support. I want to build a house for them, but I can't."

The tree replied, "I don't have a house to give you, but I have these branches you see. Take some of them and build the house you need."

The man was very happy and collected the branches to build a house for his family.

فسألته الشجرة: ما بك؟ لماذا لا تلعب معي ؟

قال: عندي مشكلة. أريد شراء أشياء كثيرة و لكن ليس معي المال لأدفع ثمنها

قالت الشجرة: خذ بعض ثمار التفاح التي على أغصاني، و اذهب و بعها في السوق و بذلك ستحصل على النقود لتشتري ما تريد

فرح الولد كثيراً بهذه الفكرة، وقام بجمع التفاح و ذهب ليبيعة و كان سعيد و مسرور جدا . و مضى وقت و لم يرجع الى الشجرة ليخبرها بما حدث معة فحزنت الشجرة كثيرا .

مرت شهور طويلة قبل أن يرجع الولد الى الشجرة و حين عاد جلس تحتها و لم يلعب معها و حين سألته عن السبب قال : أنا الآن أصبحت رجلا مسؤولا عن عائلة و أريد أن أبني لهم بيتا و لكني لا أستطيع

قالت الشجرة : أنا ليس عندي بيت لأعطيك اياه و لكن عندي الأغصان التي تراها فخذ بعضا منها و ابن البيت الذي تريد .

فرح الرجل و قام بجمع الأغصان و ذهب ليبني بيتا لعائلتة .

Many years passed, and the apple tree continued to wait for the man to return, but he did not come back. The tree waited for him for many years until he finally returned and sat under its shade.

The tree asked him, "Come play with me?" He replied, "I am an old man and I suffer from so many problems. All I want is to rest under your shade and find some peace. I want to build a boat and sail away from everyone."

The tree said, "I don't have a boat to offer you, but my trunk is strong. Take it and build the boat you need."

So the man cut a large part of the tree's trunk and used it to build his boat. Many more years went by, and he did not come back to the tree.

After a long time, the man returned to the tree. It was so used to him taking something from it every time he visited It said, "I'm sorry, I have become a very old tree and have nothing to offer you. I don't have any apples to give you to eat."

The man responded, "No need. I can't eat apples because my teeth are no longer strong enough to chew."

مرت فترة طويلة و كانت شجرة التفاح تنتظر أن يعود اليها الرجل و لكنه لم يعد و ظلت الشجرة تنتظره كثيراً، حتى عاد إليها بعد عدة سنين، وجلس تحت ظلها فطلبت منه الشجرة أن يلعب معها،

فقال : أنا رجل كبير الآن و لا أريد أن ألعب وعندي الكثير من هموم الدنيا و مشاكلها، كل ما أريد هو أن استلقي تحت ظلك وأرتاح أنا بحاجة للاسترخاء لكي أشعر بالهدوء . أريد أن أصنع مركباً وأبحر به بعيداً عن كل الناس

قالت الشجرة : ليس عندي مركبا لأقدمه لك و لكن جذعي قوي فخذه و اصنع المركب

و فعلا قام الرجل بقطع جزء كبير من جذع الشجرة وأخذه و صنع المركب الذي كان يحلم به ، ، و أيضا مرت سنين طويلة لم يذهب فيها إلى الشجرة

وبعد فترة طويلة عاد الرجل إلى الشجرة و لكن هذه المره قالت له الشجرة: أنا أسفة فقد أصبحت شجرة كبيرة، ولا أملك شيء أقدمه لك، فليس عندي تفاحاً لأعطيك إياه لتأكله

قال الرجل: لا داعي للتفاح فلن استطيع أكله بسبب أسناني، فليس عندي أسنان قوية لأ قضم بها

The tree said, "And I don't have any trunk left for you to climb."

The man laughed and said, "I'm old too and no longer able to climb."

The tree felt very sad, realizing it could no longer give him anything.

The man said, "You are still able to give. All I want now is to find comfort and peace. I want to lie down beside you and rest from the exhaustion of the world."

The tree replied, "Yes, you can rest under my shade and lie here as long as you want."

The moral of the story: Children take everything from their parents. Even after they grow up they continue to ask for more because they are used to it. When parents have given all they can and are no longer able to give more, children return to them without losing hope, knowing that true comfort and rest can only be found beside them.

قالت الشجرة: ولا أملك أي جذع لتتسلقني

فضحك الرجل وقال : لقد أصبحت عجوزاً أنا أيضاً، ولن أستطيع أن أتسلقك

شعرت الشجرة بالحزن الكبير لأنها شعرت أنها لا تستطيع أن تعطيه شيئا .

فقال لها انت دائما قادرة على العطاء و كل ما أريده الآن هو أن أشعر بالراحة والهدوء و أريد أن استلقي بجوارك لارتاح من تعب الدنيا

قالت الشجرة: إذن يمكنك النوم تحت ظلي والاستلقاء هنا كما تشاء

الحكمة المستفادة من القصة

أن الأبناء يأخذون كل شيء من والديهم حتى يكبروا ولكنهم يستمرون في الطلب لأنهم اعتادوا على ذلك وعندما يقدم الأبوان كل ما يملكان، ويصبحان غير قادرين على تقديم المزيد من العطاء، يعود الأبناء اليهم دون فقدان الأمل، وذلك لأنهم يعلمون أنه لا توجد راحة إلا بجوار والديهم

Vocabulary

Meaning	Plural	Word
Apple	تفاح	تفاحة
Branch	فروع	فرع
Bough	أغصان	غصن
Full		مليئة
Fruit	ثمار	ثمرة
Delicious		لذيذ
Trunk	جذوع	جذع
Patiently		بفارغ الصبر
Price	أثمان	ثمن
Year	سنين	سنة
Long	طوال	طويلة
Worry	هموم	همّ
Life		الدنيا

Meaning	Plural	Word
Lie down		أستلقي
Shadow	ظلال	ظل
Relax		استرخاء
Quietness		هدوء
Boat	مراكب	مركب
Sail		أبحر
Teeth	أسنان	سن
Bite		أقضم
I Own		أملك
Old man	عجائز	عجوز
Climb		يتسلق
As you wish		كما تشاء

المناقشة:

1. ماذا كان يفعل الولد كل يوم ؟

2. كيف ساعدته الشجرة في الحصول على المال ليشتري ما يريد؟

3. كيف بنى بيتا لعائلتة ؟

4. كيف ساعدتة الشجرة في بناء مركب ؟

Answer Key

جحا و العالم
Joha and the Scholar

<u>المناقشة:</u>

1. لماذا أراد العالم أن يتحدى جحا ؟ أراد العالم أن يتحدى جحا لأنه شعر بالغيرة منه
2. كم سؤالا سأل العالم جحا؟ سأل العالم جحا أربعين سؤالا
3. ما رأيك في جواب جحا؟

جحا و الشكوى
Joha and Complaining

<u>المناقشة:</u>

1. ماذا كان يعمل جحا كل ليلة ؟ كان جحا و أصحابه يجلسون معا في كل ليلة و يتحدثون
2. لماذا سئم جحا من أصحابه؟ لاحظ جحا أن أصحابه كانوا يتكلمون عن نفس المشاكل و المصاعب التي تواجههم في أعمالهم و حياتهم كل ليلة
3. ما رأيك في حل جحا لمشكلة أصحابة؟

القاضي جحا
Joha the Judge

<u>المناقشة:</u>

1. ماذا فعل الرجل الأول ؟ كان يقطع الرغيف الى قطع صغيرة و يمرر كل قطعة فوق قطع اللحم و يأكلة لأنه ليس معه مال ليشتري اللحم .
2. لماذا طلب منه صاحب الشواء المال؟ طلب منه أن يدفع ثمن رائحة اللحم
3. كم كان ثمن الشواء؟ كان ثمن الشواء خمسة دراهم
4. هل كان جحا قاضيا ذكيا؟

قصة نعل الملك
The King's Shoe

<u>المناقشة:</u>

1. لماذا قام الملك بالرحلة داخل بلده؟ اراد الملك أن يكتشف مملكته و يزور الاماكن التي فيها ويتعرف عليها

2. لماذا تورمت قدماه؟ تورمت قدماه كثيرا بسبب المشي لمسافات طويلة في الطرق الوعرة التي يصعب السير فيها،

3. ماذا قرر أن يعمل لحل هذه المشكلة؟ اصدر قرارا بتغطية جميع شوارع وطرق المملكة بالجلد، حتى لا تتأذى اقدامه و أقدام شعبة

4. ماذا اقترح علية وزيره؟ اقترح وزيره أن يحضر قطعة صغيرة من الجلد و يضعها تحت قدم الملك و قدم كل من يريد أن يمشي في المملكه

كن قدوة حسنة
Be a Good Example

المناقشة:

1. الى أين ذهب الأب مع أولاده؟ أخذ الأب طفليه إلى السيرك ليقضوا وقتا ممتعا معا

2. كم كان سعر التذاكر؟ سعر التذكرة خمسة دراهم للبالغين وثلاثة دراهم لمن هم فوق ست سنوات ومجاناً لمن هم أقل من ست سنوات

3. كم عمر أولاده ؟ واحد منهما عمره ثلاث سنوات و الثاني عمره سبع سنوات

4. هل هذا الأب قدوه حسنه؟ نعم هو قدوة حسنة جدا لأولادة

بيت للبيع
Home For Sale

المناقشة:

1. لماذا أراد الرجل أن يبيع بيته ؟ أراد الرجل أن يبيع بيته و ينتقل الى بيت أجمل من بيته

2. من الذي كتب الاعلان لبيع البيت ؟ صديق الرجل صاحب البيت هو الذي كتب الاعلان

3. كيف كان وصف البيت ؟ كان البيت في منطقة خضراء واسعة ومساحة كبيرة وله التصميم الهندسي الرائع و فيه حديقة حول البيت و أشجار كثيرة

4. لماذا غير الرجل رأيه في بيع بيته؟ بعد أن سمع وصف بيته في الاعلان قال هذا بيت رائع و كنت أحلم أن انتقل الى مثل هذا البيت، ولم أكن أدرك أن بيتي بهذا الجمال الا الآن

ثق بنفسك
Trust Yourself

المناقشة:

1. ماذا كانت تفعل الضفادع ؟ كانت هناك مجموعة ضفادع تمشي في الغابة تبحث عن الطعام و الماء

2. أين سقطت ثلاث ضفادع؟ سقطت أول ثلاث ضفادع و التي كانت تمشي في المقدمة في حفرة عميقة

3. ماذا فعل الضفدع الأول ؟ استسلم و لم يحاول الخروج

4. ماذا فعل الضفدع الثاني ؟ شعر الضفدع الثاني بالتعب و قرر أن يستسلم فنزل الى أسفل الحفرة

5. لماذا لم يستسلم الضفدع الثالث ؟ لأنه ظن أن الضفادع كانت تشجعه على الخروج بينما في الواقع كانوا يهدمون من عزيمته

هذا حال الدنيا
This is Life

المناقشة:

1. لمن زوّج الرجل ابنته الأولى ؟ تزوجت البنت الأولى من رجل فلاح و كان عنده مزرعة كبيرة

2. ماذا يعمل زوج ابنته الثانية؟ كان عنده مصنع فخار

3. ماذا طلبت منه ابنته الأولى ؟ قالت له: أدع لنا يا أبي أن تمطر الدنيا!

4. ماذا طلبت منه ابنته الثانية؟ قالت له: ادع لنا يا أبي أن لا تمطر الدنيا حتى تكون أحوالنا بخير

5. لو كنت أنت مكان هذا الأب ماذا ستفعل ؟

كما تدين تُدان
As You Condemn, You Will be Condemned

المناقشة:

1. لماذا قرر الرجل أن يأخذ أبيه الى دار المسنين؟ لان الزوجة كانت تشتكي من أبيه و تتذمر منه و أنه يحرجها بتصرفاته و ذاكرته الضعيفة أمام صديقاتها و أنه كان يكرر نفس القصة مرات عديدة كل يوم

2. ماذا أخذ معة ؟ جمع الرجل بعض الطعام والملابس و وضعها في حقيبة، ثم حمل معه قطعة كبيرة من الإسفنج لينام عليها والده هناك

3. ماذا كان يريد ابنه الصغير ؟ لماذا؟ كان يطلب من أبيه بالحاح أن يترك له نصف قطعة الاسفنج التي يحملها معه لأنه يريد أن يحتفظ بها لأبيه حين يآخذك الى دار الرعاية عندما يكبر في السن و يأتي ليسكن في بيته

4. ما رأيك في نهاية القصة؟

ساعد المحتاج
Relieve the Anxious

المناقشة:

1. من ذهب الى القرية؟ ذهب سيرك مشهور ليعمل عرض في القرية
2. كم تذكرة يحتاج المزارع للدخول الى السيرك؟ يحتاج المزارع ستة تذاكر للدخول الى السيرك
3. هل كان معه مبلغ كاف من المال؟ لا لم يكن معه مبلغ كاف من المال
4. من ساعدة ؟ ساعده الرجل الذي كان يقف خلفه

حسِن الظن
Assume Good Intentions

المناقشة:

1. ماذا لاحظ الأب ؟ لاحظ الأب أن زوج إبنته يتضايق كلما ذهبوا لزيارته و كذلك كانت تصرفات ابنته توحي أنهم غير مرتاحين بزيارتهم
2. هل لاحظت الأم ما لاحظه زوجها ؟ نعم لاحظت الأم ما لاحظة زوجها
3. ماذا قرر الأب و الأم ؟ قرر الأب و الأم أن يدعوا ابنتهم و زوجها لزيارتهم . و شعروا ان ابنتهم و زوجها يفرحون كثيرا بهذه الدعوة و جعلوها عادة أسبوعية في كل يوم جمعة
4. لماذا كان زوج البنت غير مرتاح لزيارة أهل زوجته؟ لأنه كان استدان مبلغا من المال و بدأ صاحب الدين يطالب بماله و يقول له ساتي الى بيتك لآخذ ديني ، و كان يتوقع أن يأتي في أي لحظه و هم في بيته و كان لا يريد أن يحرج نفسه أمامهم

أحب كل الناس
Love All People

المناقشة:

1. ماذا طلبت المعلمة من الطلاب في الصف ؟ طلبت المعلمة من طلابها في الفصل أن يحضروا معهم كيس فيه عدد من حبات البطاطا و أن يكتب كل طالب على كل حبة بطاطا اسم شخص يكرهه
2. ماذا كانت شروط اللعبة؟ شرط اللعبة وهو أن يحمل كل طالب كيس البطاطا معه أينما ~~ذهب لمدة أسبوع واحد فقط~~
3. لماذا فرح الأطفال بأن اللعبة انتهت ؟ الطلاب كانوا يشعرون بالتعب و يشمون رائحة كريهة تخرج من كيس البطاطا
4. ما هو هدف هذه اللعبة؟ كان الهدف هو أن تعلم الأطفال أن يسامحوا الآخرين و لا يفكروا في أخطائهم .

فكر بعقل من حولك
Think with Their Minds

المناقشة:

1. ماذا كان قرار الملك؟ أصدر قرارا يمنع فيه النساء من لبس الذهب والحلي خارج البيت

2. ماذا كانت ردة فعل النساء في البداية؟

هذا القرار لم يعجب النساء و كانت ردة الفعل كبيرة بينهن و رفضن اتباع هذا القرار لأنهن اعتدن على ذلك وبدأت النساء يتذمرن و يتحدثن مع كل من له سلطة في المملكة لايقاف هذا القرار

3. ماذا كان رأي المستشارين ؟ فقال أحدهم :أقترح التراجع عن هذا القرار حتى ترضى النساء و قال آخر : كلا إن التراجع و تغيير القرار دليل على أننا ضعفاء و نخاف منهم ويجب أن نكون أقوياء أمام الشعب حتى يتبعوا أوامرنا . وإنقسم المستشارون إلى مؤيد ومعارض

4. ما هي نصيحه الحكيم؟

أقترح أن يصدر الملك قرارا يوضح أن الجميلات فقط لا يمكنهن أن يلبس الذهب والحلى للزينه لأن الجميلات لسن بحاجة إلى الزينة و أما القبيحات فيمكنهن أن يلبسن ما يردن من الذهب و الحلي لأنهم بحاجة الى شيئ يظهر جمالهن.

5. ما رأيك في نصيحة الحكيم ؟

زرقاء اليمامة
The Blue-Eyed Yamamah

المناقشة:

1. لماذا سميت زرقاء اليمامة بهذا الاسم؟ كان هناك امرأة جميله جدا تعيش في منطقة كبيرة اسمها اليمامة أحدى مناطق السعودية . و كانت هذه المرأة عيونها زرقاء و بصرها قوي جدا و تستطيع رؤية الأشياء من مسافة بعيدة جدا . لذلك سُميت هذه المرأة "زرقاء اليمامة"

2. ماذا كانت تفعل زرقاء اليمامة لتساعد قومها؟ كانت تقف على الجبل وترى الأعداء واتجاهاتهم، ثمَّ تخبر قبيلتها كي يستعدّوا للقتال

3. لماذا أمر الملك رجاله أن يقطعوا أغصان الاشجار و يحملوها؟ أمر الملك رجاله أن يقطعوا أغصان الاشجار و يحملوها على رؤوسهم ليخدعوا زرقاء اليمامة،

4. ماذا فعل الملك بزرقاء اليمامة ؟ قلع الملك عينيها؛ لتجنب خطرها وأمر بصلبها على باب المدينة

قدّر ما تملك
Appreciate What You Have

١. ماذا كانت المشكله الكبيرة لهذا الولد ؟ كانت مشكلته أنه حين يمسك شطائره و ينظر اليها يجدها باردة بلا طعم ولا رائحة و لا يشعر بالجوع فكان يتركها في الكيس

٢. كيف كان يأكل زميله في المدرسة ؟ كان يأكلها و هو مستمتعا بها جدا

٣. كيف كانت المدرسة الجديدة؟ كانت المعلمة الجديدة تتحدث مع الطلاب و تحترم رأيهم كأنهم بالغين . لقد كانت تعاملهم كأنهم أبناؤها و كانت تبتسم دائمًا

٤. كيف كانت ساندويشات زميله ؟ عادية جدا وليس لها طعم مختلف كما كان يعتقد

٥. ماذا تعلمت من هذه القصة ؟ ما دمنا نراقب الناس من حولنا فلن تستمع بما نملك أو بما نحضره.

الثعلب و الثعبان
The Fox and The Snake

المناقشة :

١. لماذا حمل الرجل الثعبان و وضعه تحت ملابسة؟ الرجل أشفق عليه و حمله و وضعه تحت فانيلته ليدفئه

٢. كيف كان الطقس؟ كان الطقس باردا جدا

٣. لماذا لا يريد الثعبان أن يخرج من تحت ملابس الرجل؟ لأنه يريد أن يبقى تحت فانيلته لأنه مكان دافئ

٤. ماذا كانت ستفعل الأفعى لو أخرجها الرجل من تحت ملابسة؟ قالت له الأفعى :اذا حاولت اخراجي من هنا فسوف أعضك و ستموت في الحال .

٥. لماذا ذهب الرجل الى الثعلب ؟ لأنه يريد حلا ليخرج الثعبان من تحت ملابسه

٦. لو كنت أنت مكان هذا الرجل هل ستساعد الثعبان ؟

الحياة لا تخلو من المشاكل
Everyone Has Their Own Problems.

المناقشة:

١. لماذا كان الرجل الفقير يتحسر على حياة جاره ؟ كان يتحسرفي قلبه لأنه لا يملك مثل جاره .

٢ ماذا رأى في بيت جارة و أهميه ؟زار ٣١ (١٦ ، ٣ أشهام) ؟تأمل بالحديقة الكبيرة و بالاشجار المتنوعة ذات الثمار الكثيرة و الأزهار المختلفة الألوان و السيارات المتنوعة و صار يفكر هذه هي الجنّة بعينها . ثم دخل الى المنزل و بدأ يتأمل في الصالة الكبيرة و الغرف الواسعة و كل الأثاث الفخم و الجميل الموجود فيها .

3. ماذا كان طعام الرجل الغني؟ لماذا؟ كان يأكل الخبز اليابس لأنه كان يعاني من المرض و أنه لا يستطيع أن يأكل هذا الطعام اللذيذ و أن الطبيب قال له ان بامكانه أن يأكل الخبز الناشف فقط

4. في رأيك ما هو الأفضل أن تكون غنيا و مريضا أو فقيرا و بصحة جيدة؟

استمتع بقهوتك
Enjoy Your Coffee

المناقشة:

1. من الذين دعاهم الأستاذ الى بيته؟ دعا الأستاذ لبيته مجموعة من طلابه السابقين و كان هؤلاء الطلاب قد حققوا الاستقرار المادي و نجحوا في حياتهم العملية وكانوا يعملون في مراكز عالية

2. عن ماذا بدأ يتحدث الخريجون ؟ بدأوا يتحدثون عن الضغوطات التي يواجهونها في أعمالهم و يشكون من حياتهم و عملهم الكثير لأنه يسبب لهم الكثير من التوتر .

3. ماذا تمثل القهوة؟ القهوة تمثل الحياة

4. ماذا تمثل الفناجين ؟ تمثل الفناجين الوظيفة و المال .

5. ما رأيك في كلام الأستاذ ؟

العقل ليس بالسن
Maturity Does Not Have an Age

المناقشة:

1. لماذا استغرب موظفي البنك؟ كان هناك ولد صغير يذهب الى البنك كل أسبوع و يضع 500 جنيه في حسابه، إستغرب الموظفون كيف يحصل على هذا المال و هو مبلغ كبير لولد في مثل عمره

2. من أين يأخذ الولد المال؟ كان كل يوم يراهن الناس في الشارع و يكسب الرهان.

3. كيف قبّل الولد عينه ؟ أخرج العدسات من عينيه و قبلها ثم وضعها في عينيه

4. على ماذا راهن الولد في المرة الثانية؟ راهن الموظفين العشرة على أنة سيجعل المدير ينزع بنطاله

5. ما رأيك في هذا الولد؟

القاضي الذكي والشجرة المتكلمة
The Smart Judge and the Talking Tree

المناقشة:

1. لماذا خرج علاء و زاهر ؟ كان الشابان في رحلة تجارية

2. ماذا وجد علاء ؟ وجد كيسا من المال فأخذه

3. لو كنت أنت من وجد كيس المال هل ستخبر صاحبك عنه؟

4. ما هو موقف أبو زاهر ؟ أبو زاهر مخادع و كاذب مثل ابنه

5. كيف تصرف القاضي ؟ أراد أن يعلم زاهر درسا لا ينساه وأمر بارجاع كل المال الى علاء وجلد زاهر ووالده عقابا لهم.

الأميرة والفقير
The Princess and the Poor Man

المناقشة:

1. كيف كانت الأميرة تعامل الخدم؟ كانت مغرورة و تعامل الخدم بقسوة و تحتقرهم . و كانت لا تحترم مشاعرهم و تصرخ عليهم باستمرار.

2. هل كان والدها يحب تصرفاتها؟ لا . والدها غضب منها و جلس يتحدث معها و طلب منها ان لا تعيد ذلك و أنه اذا سمعها تصرخ على الخدم مرة أخرى فانه لن يسمح لها أن تبقى في القصر

3. ماذا فعل الملك ليعلمها كيف تغير تصرفها؟ صمم أن يزوّجها للشاب الفقير.

4. هل كان زوجها فقير؟ لا و لكنه كان أميرا مثلها

5. ما رأيك في خطة الملك؟

ليلى والذئب
Layla and the Wolf

المناقشة:

1. ماذا كانت تحمل ليلى في يدها؟ سلة بها بعض الطعام و كعك وأعشاب طبية لجدتها

2. لماذا ذهبت ليلى في طريق الغابة؟ لأنها تريد أن تجمع الزهور الملونة

3. كيف وصلت ليلى الى بيت جدتها؟ من ساعدها؟ الصياد ساعدها و أخذها الي بيت جدتها .

4. بماذا نصحها الصياد؟ أوصى ليلى أن تستمع الى والدتها دائما .

الوالد و الابن
Father and Son

المناقشة:

1. لماذا كان الولد ينتظر أبيه عند باب البيت؟ لأنه يريد أن يعرف كم يتبض في الساعة الواحدة

2. لماذا غضب الأب ؟ غضب الأب كثيرا لأن هذا ليس الوقت المناسب ليطلب ابنه منه بعض المال ليشتري لعبة أو أي شيئ

3. هل أعطى الأب ابنة ما يريد من النقود؟ نعم أعطى الأب ابنه ما يريد من النقود

4. ماذا يريد الابن أن يشتري ؟ يريد الأبن أن يشتري ساعة من وقت أبيه

5. ما رأيك في تصرف الابن؟ تصرف ذكي

جزاء سنمار
Sinmar's Reward

المناقشة:

1. لماذا أراد النعمان أن يبني قصرا ؟ أراد أن يبني قصرا عظيما، يباهي به جميع الملوك في ذلك الوقت، ويفاخرهم.

2. هل أعجب الملك القصر ؟ نعم أعجب الملك ببناء القصر كثيرا

3. هل هناك بنّاء غير سنمار يستطيع أن يبني مثل هذا القصر؟ لا لم يكن هناك أي بنّاء يستطيع أن يبني قصرا مثل سنمار

4. ماذا كانت جائزة سنمار ؟ أمر الملك جنوده أن يلقوا سنمار من فوق سطح القصرو سقط سنمار من هذا الإرتفاع الكبير على سطح الأرض، ومات في الحال

5. لماذا قرر الملك قتل سنمار ؟ قرر الملك قتل سنمار حتى لا يبني أي قصر آخر مثل قصر الملك

القانون لا يحمي المغفلين
The Law Doesn't Protect the Fool

المناقشة:

1. ماذا اشترى التاجر الخبيث بدرهمين ؟ أشتري الحصان و كل ما يحمله من الحطب بدرهمين

2. ماذا حكم القاضي في المرة الأولى ؟ حكم القاضي باعطاء الحصان للتاجر

3. لماذا استأجر الحطاب حصانا؟ استأجر الحطال حصانا ليذهب و يحتطب لأنه لا يملك المال ليشتري حصانا آخر

4. لماذا أخرجت الفتاة سكينا من جيبها؟ لأنها كانت تريد أن تقطع يد التاجر ثمنا للحطب

5. كم دفع التاجر لينقذ نفسة ؟ دفع التاجر الف درهم لينقذ يده و نفسه

6. ما رأيك بتفكير الفتاة؟

جبينة
Jobaina

المناقشة:

1. ماذا دعت الأم ؟ دعت الأم أن يرزقها الله بنت جميله و بيضاء مثل الجبنة .

2. لماذا سمت ابنتها جبينه؟ لأنها كانت بيضاء مثل الجبنه

3. أين ذهبت جبينه مع صديقاتها؟ ذهبت الى القرية المجاورة لتشارك في العرس

4. ماذا حدث لخرزة جبينة؟ وقعت الخرزة منها في النهر

5. هل هناك خرزة سحرية؟ لا أعتقد

6. ماذا تشبه الخرزة في عصرنا الحاضر ؟ انها مثل التلفون

ستحصد ما تزرع
You Will Reap What You Sow

<u>المناقشة:</u>

1. ماذا كان يعمل محمد؟ كان محمد يعمل ساقيا

2. لماذا أراد الملك أن يعمل محمد ساقيا عنده في القصر؟ حتى يستمتع الملك و من معه بالقصر بقصصه وحكاياته و كلامه الجميل

3. لماذا أراد الوزير أن يتخلص من محمد؟ كانت علاقة محمد بالملك تجعل الوزير يغار كثيرا من محمد و أخذ يفكر في خدعة حتى يبعده عن الملك

4. لماذا لبس محمد لثاما على وجهه؟ لبس محمد اللثام ليحمي الملك من رائحة فمة الكريهة

5. لماذا غضب الملك من محمد؟ غضب الملك لأن الوزير قال له أن محمد يشتكي من رائحة فمة الكريهة و هو يضع اللثام حتى لا يشمها .

6. ما رأيك في نهاية القصة ؟

الفتى وشجرة التفاح
The Apple Tree and the Boy

<u>المناقشة:</u>

1. ماذا كان يفعل الولد كل يوم ؟
كان يقضي طوال اليوم يصعد فوق شجرة التفاح و يجري حولها و يأكل من ثمرها حين يجوع و ينام تحت ظلها حين يشعر بالتعب

2. كيف ساعدته الشجرة في الحصول على المال ليشتري ما يريد؟ قالت له لأن يأخذ بعض ثمار التفاح التي على أغصانها، و يذهب و يبيعها لمن يريد و بذلك سيحصل على النقود ليشتري ما يريد

3. كيف بنى بيتا لعائلتة ؟ قالت له الشجرة أن يأخذ الأغصان التي عليها و يبني بها البيت

4. كيف ساعدتة الشجرة في بناء مركب ؟ قالت له ان جذعها قوي فأخذه و صنع المركب

English-Arabic Glossary

A

Accept ترضى

Accuracy الدقة

Achieved حقق

Achievements انجاز / انجازات

Actually بالفعل

Added أضاف

Adornments الحلي

Advertise تنشر

Advertisement إعلان

Advised أوصى

Advisor مستشار / مستشارون

Allow تسمح

Alone بمفردك

Although مع أن

And so on و هكذا

Animal حيوان حيوانات

Annoyed, bothered يتضايق

Annoying مزعجا

Another أخرى

Apple تفاحة / تفاح

Appreciate قدّر

Architectural معماري

Armenian آرمي

Army جيش / جيوش

Arrogant مغرور / مغرورين

As long as ما دام

As you wish كما تشاء

Asking for يطالب

At this time عندئذ

Attention اهتمام

Axe فأس / فؤوس

B

Bad سيئة

Bag كيس / أكياس

Barbequing يشوي

Barn حظيرة / حظائر

Basket سلة / سلال

Be harsh تقسو

Bead خرزة / خرزات

Beard لحية

Beauty جمال

Became closer اقترب

Became very tired ضاق ذرعاً

Bed سرير / أسرة

Beg توسل

Beginning مقدمة

Behavior تصرف / تصرفات

Believe يصدق

Bemoan يتحسر

Beside me بجواري

Beside بجانبه

Better أفضل

Between بين

Bite يعض / أقضم

Bite you أعضك

Black soot سخام أسود

Blessings نِعمة / نِعَم

Blue زرقاء

Boat مركب / مراكب

Borrow تقترض

Both of you كلاكما

Bothered يتأذى

Bough غصن / أغصان

Bouquet باقة / باقات

Boy ولد / أولاد

Brag يفاخر

Branch غصن / أغصان

Bread خبز

Breakfast فطور

Bride عروس / عرايس

Builder بنّاء / بنّائين

Businessman رجل أعمال

Butler ساقي / سقاة

Buy أشتري

C

Cake كعكة / كعك

Calculate يحسب

Calling ينادي

Camel ناقة / نوق

Challenge يتحدى

Chance فرصة / فرص

Change his mind تراجع

Chaos يتّراجع

Cheater مخادع

Cheer يهتف

Cheese جبنة

Child طفل / أطفال

Choice خيار / خيارات

Choose اختار

Circus سيرك

Cleaning تنظيف

Climb يتسلق

Close قريب

Closed أغلق

Cold بارد

Colleague زميل / زملاء

Colorful ملونة

Come تعال

Come to mind على بال / يخطر

Complain يشكي / يشكون

Condition شرط / شروط

Confidence ثقة

Continue تستمر

Cooking طبخ

Corner ركن / أركان

Countryside ريف / أرياف

Cover تغطية

Crucify صلب

Cruel خبيث / خبثاء

Cry يبكي

Culture العادة

Cunning محتال

Cup فنجان / فناجين

Customer زبون / زبائنه

Cut a piece أقتطع

Cut the wood يحتطب

D

Dance يرقص

Dangerous خطيرة

Dare يتجرأ

Deaf أصم

Debt دين / ديون

Deceive يوهم

Decision قرار / قرارات

Deep عميقة

Delete, erase محا

Delicious لذيذ

Deltoid دالية

Desert صحراء

Deserve يستحق / تستحق

Design صمم

Died مات

Difficulty صعوبة / مصاعب

Dinar دينار / دنانير

Dinner عشاء

Direct مباشرة

Directly مباشرة

Disaster مصيبة / مصائب

Discontent استياء

Discover يكتشف

Disease مرض / أمراض

Dish or plate صحن

Double ضعف / أضعاف

Doubt الظن

Doubt شك / شكوك

Drape ستارة / ستائر

Dry / hard يابس

E

Eagerness شوق

Earn تقبض

Elder مسن / مسنين

Elementary الابتدائية

Embarrassed تتحرج

Embarrassment حرج

Emergency طارئ / طوارئ

Employee موظف / موظفون

Encourage يشجع

Enemy عدو / أعداء

Engineer مهندس / مهندسين

Engineering design تصميم هندسي

Enjoy يتمتع / يستمتع

Enjoyable ممتعا

Evidence دليل

Example قدوة

Exception إستثناءً / استثناءات

Exceptional مميز

Exchange تبادل

Expected توقعت

Expensive غالية

Expert خبير

F

Factory مصنع / مصانع

Famous مشهور / مشهورين

Farm مزرعة / مزارع

Farmer مزارع / مزارعين /

فلاح / قلاحين

Feel happy فرح

Felt bad أشفق

Find أجد

Finished انتهت

Flogged جلد

Flowers زهرة / زهور / تابع / أتباع

Foot قدم / أقدام

For trade للتجارة

Forest غابة / غابات

Forgive يسامح

Foul كريهة / نتنة

Found وجد

Fox ثعلب / ثعالب

Free مجانا

Friday جمعة

Friend صاحب / أصحاب

Frog صفدع / صفادع

Fruit حبة / حبات / ثمرة / ثمار

Full مليئة

G

Game لُعبة / لُعَب

Garden حديقة / حدائق

Get a debt استدان

Get married تزوج

Get over التغلب

Get pregnant تحمل

Get ready يستعد

Get rid of التخلص

Give birth ولدت

Give me ارزقني

Gives the impression توحي

Go up صعد

Goal هدف / أهداف

Gold الذهب

Got إنزعج

Got tired of something سئم

Gouge قلع

Graduate خريج / خريجين

Gradually تدر ج / الطريقة

Gratitude امتنان

Great عظيم / عظماء

Greedy طماع

Green خضراء

Greet her يحيونها

Greetings تحية

Groom عريس / عرسان

Group مجموعة / مجموعات

Guests ضيف / ضيوف

Gun بندقية / بنادق

H

Habit عادة / عادات

Happen تحدث

Happened حدث

Happiness فرح / أفراح

Happy سعيد / سعداء

Hard قاسي / قُساه

Hardship مشقة / مشقات

Harm تتأذى

Hat قبعة / قبعات

Hate يكره

Hateful كريهة

He stopped him استوقفه

Head cutter (using a sword) السياف

Heart قلب

Held me أمسكني

Help يساعد

Helper مساعد / مساعدون

Her suggestion اقتراحها

Heralds, tells good news يبشر

Herbal عشبة / أعشاب

Hide توارى

His account حساب

His undershirt فانيلته

History تاريخ

Hold عقد

Hole حفرة / حفر

Honest أمين

Honestly بصراحة

Hope أمل / آمال

Horse حصان / أحصنة

Hour ساعة / ساعات

Human being إنسان

Humans بشر

Humble متواضع / متواضعون

Hunger جوع

Hunter صياد / صيادين

I

I am honored يشرفني

I bet أراهن

I borrowed استدنت

I kiss أُقبّل

I know أعرف

I liked أعجبتني

I own أملك

I think أعتقد

I win أكسب

I wish أتمنى

I won كسبت

Idea فكرة

Imagine أتخيّل

Immediately على الفور / في الحال

Implement تنفيذ

Impossible مستحيل

Injustice ظلم

Insist مصمم

Insisted صمم

Insistence إلحاح

Intuitiveness بديهه

Invitation دعوة / دعوات

Invite دعى

Issued أصدر

J

Jealousy غيرة

Job عمل / أعمال

Judge قاضي / قضاه

Jumped قفز

Jungle ادغال

K

Kettle ابريق / أباريق

Kill قتل

Kind طيب

Kind, type نوع / أنواع

King ملكا / ملوك

Kingdom مملكة / ممالك

Knife سكين / سكاكين

Knocked طرق

Know يعرف / يعرفون

L

Lady سيدة / سيدات

Land أرض / أراض

Late متأخر / متأخرين / تأخر

Laugh ضحك

Leather جلد / جلود

Leave ينصرف / تغادر

Leaving مغادرة

Left يسار

Lend me تعيرني

Lenses عدسة / العدسات

Less أقل

Let me know اعلمني

Let's دعنا

Liar كاذب

Lie down أستلقي

Life الحياة / الدنيا

Like it, same مثيل

Line صف / صفوف

Loaf رغيفاً / أرغفة

Location موقع

Long طويلة / طوال

Look down تحتقر

Lunch غداء

Luxurious فخمة

Luxury رفاهية

M

Magical سحرية

Make fun of يسخر

Manager مدير / مدراء

Many كثيرا

Marketing تسويق

Mask لثام

Mattress فراش

Mature بالغ / بالغين

Means وسيلة / وسائل

Meat لحم

Medical طبية

Meeting اجتماع / اجتماعات

Memory ذكرى / ذكريات

Minister وزير / وزراء

Minister سلطة / سلطات

Misery شقاء

Money مال

Month شهر / أشهر

More مزيد

Mother أم / أمهات / والدة / والدات

Mountain جبل / جبال

Move ينتقل

Musical instrument آلة موسيقية / الات موسيقية

N

Nature طبيعة

Newspaper الجريدة

Next تالي

Night ليلة / ليال

Nighttime ليلا

Not your business ليس من شأنك

Noticed لاحظ

O

Occasion مناسبة / مناسبات

Oh God يا رب

Old man عجوز / عجائز

Old times قديم الزمان

Opinion رأي / آراء

Opponent معارض / معارضون

Order أمر / أوامر

Ordered him أمره

Organized مرتب

Others آخر

Own تملك

P

Palace قصر / قصور

Pants بنطال / بنطلونات

Pass it أ مرر

Patiently بفارغ الصبر

Pay يدفع

People شعب / شعوب
Persevere تحمّل
Person شخص / أشخاص
Petty الشفقة
Pie, sandwich شطيرة
Pillow مخدة / مخدات
Plan خطة / خطط
Plate طبق / أطباق
Plot يكيد
Pointed at أشار
Poisonous سام
Police شرطي / شرطة
Popular محبوب
Position مركز / مراكز
Potato بطاطا
Pottery فخار
Pour يسكبْ
Practical العملية
Prepare يعد
Pretend اظهر
Price ثمن / أثمان / سعر / أسعار
Problem مشكلة / مشاكل
Productive مثمرة
Prohibit يمنع
Protest احتجاج / احتجاجات
Prove يثبت

Q

Question سؤال / أسئلة
Questioning استغراب
Quietness هدوء

R

Rain مطر / أمطار

Reaction ردة فعل / ردود فعل
Realized أدركت
Reason سبب / أسباب
Refused رفضت
Regrated ندم
Relax استرخاء / يرتاح
Remember تذكر
Remembering استعادة
Rented إستأجر
Repeated متكررة
Repetition تكرار
Respect احترام
Response اجابة
Result نتيجة / نتنائج
Retire تقاعد
Retract التراجع
Reward أكافئ / جائزة
Rich ثري / أثرياء
Right يمين
Ringing رنين
River نهر / أنهار
Road طريق / طرق
Robe رداء
Roof سطح
Rough path الوعرة
Rub يفرك
Rule يحكم

S

Safe أمان
Sail أبحر
Salesperson بائع – بائعة
Same نفس
Sand تراب

Save it أبقيه

Save توفر

Scared نخاف

Scholar عالِم / علماء

Season شتاء

Secret سر / أسرار

Secretly خفية

See رؤية

Seed بذرة / بذور

Selfish أناني / أنانيون

Sell يبيع / يبيع

Sentence عبارة / عبارات

Servant خادم / خدم

Shadow ظل / ظلال

She begged توسَّلت

She regrets نادمة

Sheep غنم / أغنام

Shepard ترعى

Shiver يرتجف

Shock ذهول

Shocked مصدوما / تفاجأ

Show عرض / عروض

Showing off يباهي

Side جانب / جوانب

Sight بصر / أبصار

Sign مؤشر / مؤشرات

Significance مغزى

Simple بسيطة

Sing يغني

العال ١١١١١١١١١١

Smell رائحة / روائح

Smiled ابتسم

Snake ثعباناً - أفعى

Solution حل / حلول

Some بعض

Son ابن / أبناء

Special خاصّة

Spoiled مدلل / مدللين

Sponge الإسفنج

Stole سلب

Stomach معدة

Store دكان / دكاكين

Story قصة / قصص

Strange غريب / غرباء

Street شارع / شوارع

Stress توتر / ضغط / ضغوطات

Student طالب / طلاب / تلميذ / تلاميذ

Submit استسلم

Suddenly فجأة

Suggest أقترح

Sultan سلطان / سلاطين

Summoned استدعى

Supporter مؤيد / مؤيدون

Surprised مستغربا

Sweat عرق

Swollen تورمت

T

Take off خلع

Taking care of رعاية

Taste طعم

Teach يلقن

Teacher (female) معلمة / معلمات

Teeth ... / أسنان

Testify تشهد

Thank حمد

The area منطقة / مناطق

The bank البنك / البنوك

The bet الرهان

The case القضية / قضايا

The rest باقي

Their story قصتهم

Then ثم

Threaten يهدد

Throw him ألقوه

Ticket seller قاطع التذاكر

Ticket تذكرة / تذاكر

Tired متعب / متعبين

To spend ليقضوا

To warm ليدفئة

Together معا

Told حكى

Too أيضاً

Top أعلى

Topic موضوع / موضوعات

Trace أثر

Travel يسافر

Travelling مسافر / مسافرون

Tray صينية / صواني

Tree شجرة / أشجار

Trial محاولة / محاولات

Tribe قبيلة / قبائل

Trip رحلة / رحلات

Triumph انتصار / انتصارات

Trunk جذع / جذوع

Trying يحاول

T-shirt قميص / قمصان

Two tickets تذكرتين

U

Ugly قبيحة / قبيحات

Underwear ملابسك الداخلية

Use the bathroom يقضي حاجته

Used to اعتاد

V

Village قرية / قرى

Visit يزور

W

Waiting ينتظر

Wander يتجوّل

War حرب / حروب

Warm دافئ

Washing غسل

We burry ندفن

We Pray ندعوا

Weak ضعيف / ضعفاء

Weather طقس

Wedding عرس أعراس

Week أسبوع أسابيع

Went around طاف

When حين

Whenever كلما

Wherever أينما

Wide فسيحة

Wide واسعة

Will compensate us سيعوضنا

Will lose سنفقد

Will pollute ستلوث

Wise حكيم / حكماء

Wisper همس

Witness يشهد / يشهدوا

Witnesses شاهد / الشهود

Wolf ذئب / ذئاب

Woman امرأة / نساء

Wondering تساؤل / تساؤلات
Wood حطب
Wood cutter حطاب
Worry قلق
Written مكتوبا

Y

Year سنة / سنوات
Yesterday البارحة / أمس
Young guy شاب
Your majesty جلالتك / جلالتكم
Youth شاب / شباب

Audio Track List

How to access the audio recordings for this book:

1. Check to be sure you have an Internet connection.
2. Type the URL below into your web browser.

https://www.tuttlepublishing.com/arabic-folktales-for-language-learners

For support you can email us at info@tuttlepublishing.com.

"Books to Span the East and West"

Tuttle Publishing was founded in 1832 in the small New England town of Rutland, Vermont [USA]. Our core values remain as strong today as they were then—to publish best-in-class books which bring people together one page at a time. In 1948, we established a publishing outpost in Japan—and Tuttle is now a leader in publishing English-language books about the arts, languages and cultures of Asia. The world has become a much smaller place today and Asia's economic and cultural influence has grown. Yet the need for meaningful dialogue and information about this diverse region has never been greater. Over the past seven decades, Tuttle has published thousands of books on subjects ranging from martial arts and paper crafts to language learning and literature—and our talented authors, illustrators, designers and photographers have won many prestigious awards. We welcome you to explore the wealth of information available on Asia at www.tuttlepublishing.com.

Published by Tuttle Publishing, an imprint of Periplus Editions (HK) Ltd.

www.tuttlepublishing.com

Copyright ©2025 Sarah Risha

Library of Congress Catalog-in-Publication Data in progress

ISBN 978-0-8048-5710-9

First edition
28 27 26 25 24
10 9 8 7 6 5 4 3 2 1   2411VP

Printed in Malaysia

TUTTLE PUBLISHING® is a registered trademark of Tuttle Publishing, a division of Periplus Editions (HK) Ltd.

Distributed by

North America, Latin America & Europe
Tuttle Publishing
364 Innovation Drive, North Clarendon
VT 05759-9436 U.S.A.
Tel: 1 (802) 773-8930
Fax: 1 (802) 773-6993
info@tuttlepublishing.com
www.tuttlepublishing.com

Japan
Tuttle Publishing
Yaekari Building 3rd Floor
5-4-12 Osaki Shinagawa-ku
Tokyo 141 0032
Tel: (81) 3 5437-0171
Fax: (81) 3 5437-0755
sales@tuttle.co.jp
www.tuttle.co.jp

Asia Pacific
Berkeley Books Pte. Ltd.
3 Kallang Sector #04-01
Singapore 349278
Tel: (65) 6741-2178 Fax: (65) 6741-2179
inquiries@periplus.com.sg
www.tuttlepublishing.com